"Brandon Pope writes with great credibility not simply because he understands Wall Street but because he has discovered the financial principles that transcend man's wisdom. Read his timely book to gain God's wisdom and experience true wealth."

— Chuck Bentley, CEO
Crown Financial Ministries

"*Spiritual lessons from Wall Street* is a fast read, and full of very practical concepts that illustrate that… 'The more we give, the more we realize we can live without.'"

— Sam Gilliland, Chairman & CEO
Sabre Holdings

"*Spiritual lessons from Wall Street* is a journey that transforms the status quo of success. By his example, Brandon Pope will challenge you to find fulfillment through a powerful spiritual lens. Be prepared to take action after this read!"

— Catherine F. Rohr, Founder & CEO
Prison Entrepreneurship Program

"Affluence is a tricky thing. It's rarely correlated to fulfillment. I see people all the time whose bank accounts are exceeded in size only by the vacuum of emptiness in their hearts. There is a reason for that, and Brandon Pope has figured it out. I love the insights in this book."

— Paul Rasmussen, Pastor – Cornerstone Community
Highland Park United Methodist Church

"Brandon's transparent journey confronts timeless questions about life's earthly priorities while offering a path....and a challenge... for significance and meaning through spiritual learning and service."

— Norm Bagwell

"'We make a living by what we get, we make a life by what we give.' Sir Winston Churchill may have said it first, but *Spiritual lessons from Wall Street* puts real feet to those words with pointed practicality. Brandon Pope employs his wealth and depth of knowledge to transform your financial perspective and purpose. A spiritual and financial paradigm shift are in your future after completing this book."

— Zoë P. Elmore, Nationally Known Speaker and Author
Proverbs 31 Ministries

Spiritual lessons from
WALL STREET

A personal journey of financial security, emotional bankruptcy and spiritual uncertainty

Brandon Pope

Brian, I love you & God Bless!

IPG

Intermedia Publishing Group

Spiritual lessons from WALL STREET

Published by:
Intermedia Publishing Group
P.O. Box 2825
Peoria, Arizona 85380
www.intermediapub.com

ISBN 978-0-9819682-1-6

Table of Contents

Introduction & Acknowledgments

I didn't set out to write a book. But it needed to be written. In a nutshell, it needed to be written for those of us who struggle to achieve the American dream or have achieved it, and at the same time, find that dream in conflict with God's dream for each and every one of us, God's mission to love one another and love Him.

I set out late one night, in the mission fields of Juarez, Mexico—after a long day spent with the poorest of the poor—to reconcile what I do for a living. As a financial advisor for the wealthiest of the wealthy, I had accomplished more financially than I had dreamed possible. I had carved out a very secure life for myself, and now I was face to face with extreme poverty. How could I reconcile what I had accomplished financially, what I knew about wealth in America and around the world, with the pain and suffering I was witnessing?

My problem was that I had it. This so-called American dream. I achieved it. I enjoyed it. But I was still empty. I still had a void. A hole. Financially secure. Emotionally bankrupt. Spiritually uncertain. Which is how I ended up in Juarez, Mexico. I needed to experience this poverty firsthand. I searched it out, in hopes of finding meaning. Meaning for life. Meaning for my family. Meaning for the empty feeling in the pit of my stomach. Having everything, felt like having nothing at all.

And there was no escaping it.

To reconcile these feelings, my faith and my struggles with the very success that many of us strive and spend lifetimes achieving, I knew I had to do something about it. I knew *that* with every fiber of my being, without quite knowing what *that* was.

Sometimes spiritual lessons are found in the last place you would expect.

And *that,* as you'll find, can be found within the pages of this book.

Without this book and the incredible journey it took me on, I'm not sure I would have survived the horrific economic environment of 2008–2009. Today's financial times—the economy, layoffs, the falling stock markets, the credit crisis, a possible depression looming—can scare the American dream right out of you.

Thankfully, amid the journey of reconciling my own struggles with success and faith, I have weathered these tough times mentally, emotionally and spiritually. I have a renewed sense of well-being, a sense of God's joy and grace rising from *what I have*, rather than what I don't, what God provided for me and my family, rather than what might have been lost in the markets.

Obtaining a clear picture of God's direction and plan for me throughout the writing of this book, allowed me to shift focus from myself to others. Those in need. Those in pain. Those suffering. Not just the poor...but the rich as well. My clients. My neighborhood. My community.

Being a financial advisor for 20+ years of 100 or so of the wealthiest families in the U.S., having spent 12+ of those years with one of the premier Wall Street firms, I see a different side of wealth. A struggle, a passion, a fear, a possession. And these were experiences I wanted to share. With that said, these experiences are not client specific, rather a consensus and sanitized composite of the types of meetings, conversations and thoughts that I dealt with in the trenches of Wall Street. Our relationships, our meetings, our discussions with clients are private and confidential. And this privacy is retained within these pages. No story, no paragraph, no commentary regarding my clients or my business experiences by itself is a summary of any individual meeting or conversation. Rather, articulate examples of the type of conversations that have been the lifeline of a very personal relationship I enjoy and am blessed to have with these families. Their struggles, their pain, their search for the true meaning of life are no different from my own.

A book is never written in a vacuum. Thankfully this book is no exception.

First and foremost, I thank God. I know that sounds typical of a Christian author, but I truly have a lot to be thankful for, and I owe it all to Him. Not long ago, my life was focused solely, squarely on me and my family. God has steered my life in a direction where there's no turning back.

God has placed individuals in my life that I could not live without, in Heaven or on earth. To start with, my wife, Maria. My true partner. A miracle. A loving, caring, passionate wife filled with grace, peace, direction and encouragement. You've guided me, counseled me and brought me along from the depths I reached, to the mountains, and all the space in between. I am lucky. I am blessed. I owe it all to you. I love you.

To my children, Jackson and Rachel, who I adore and cherish. I am humbled in my role in stewarding and shaping your lives in Christ. If this book sells only two copies, I would want those copies in your hands. And that would be enough. My mistakes and successes are written all over these pages, and I hope you carry this passion for others as you live out your mission in life.

To my church home, Highland Park United Methodist, and the many opportunities and individuals within those walls, to experience faith, service and mission. Many of the service and mission opportunities expressed in this book came from your tireless efforts to provide members in Christ a chance to get out and live our faith. Although the church is a true community— and it is that community of Christ that I thank—I lift up Paul Rasmussen, Pastor–Cornerstone Community and Rev. Mark Craig, Senior Minister.

To my employer and partner, Bernstein Global Wealth Management, a unit of AllianceBernstein L.P., for being a firm built on a solid foundation of integrity, collaboration, professionalism, transparency, honesty, client orientation and commitment. A firm with unmatched ethics, technical skills and empathy for our clients and their goals and objectives. A firm that I am proud of, and always will be proud of, for the mark they made within an industry in need of repair.

To those early readers, reviewers and commentators of this work, I wholeheartedly thank you for the time and willingness to read an early draft. Without your input, this book would have never made it this far. You know who you are, however, I lift up by name Paige McDaniel, Tom Lueder, Shannon Gilliland, Zoë Elmore and Neil Moseley.

To my editor, Timothy S. Miller, I owe grateful appreciation for encouragement, enthusiasm and dedication to the work you discovered within the various journal writings I carried endlessly. You're an individual with great faith and direction, who experienced the battles depicted within this book first hand, and who dealt with the on again, off again nature of this work. I thank you from the bottom of my heart.

To Intermedia Publishing, Larry Davis and W. Terry Whalin, I say thanks for the entrepreneurial attitude and spirit with which you faithfully approach authors, and the publishing business as a whole. Your tireless efforts brought this vision home and delivered on your promises.

I pass along my love and thanks to my family outside of Texas. Ralph, I love you, I'm proud of you and thank you for being my father. Barbara, I love you, I cry for you, I long for the mom I knew earlier in life and I look forward to reconnecting with you later in eternity. Brian, my older brother, I love you, I care for you and I miss you. We have drifted apart, and I want to mend those fences. Lanie, my little sister, I love you, I can't do without you and I'm sorry. I'm sorry it's taken me so long to realize what a gift you are to me and those around you. Lois, I love you. You are a gift. To me, a gift to your daughters, a gift to your late husband Nick and a gift of service and mission to those you touch. Zoe and Tom, I love each of you, and value the Christ-led household each of you exhibit and model to those around you.

And the many folks who have not been named but have shown their love and support in more ways than could possibly be recognized, I thank you.

"I know plenty of people, both rich and poor, who are suffocating from the weight of the American dream, who find themselves heavily burdened by the lifeless toil and consumption we put upon ourselves."[1]

— Shane Claiborne, The Irresistible Revolution

1

I've Got It All...Now What?

LESSON: Greed *for God* **is Good**

Greed is good. Or so said Gordon Gekko, the slick, greedy, money-loving Wall Street executive played by Michael Douglas in the 1987 film *Wall Street*. I loved it. I soaked it up. I idolized that way of life. That fast-paced environment. That world. Money. Fame. Fast cars. Luxurious homes. Designer clothes. Easy Street. The American dream.

And while the fictional world of *Wall Street* played out on the big screen, I was an impressionable college student busy learning how to make money. How to produce earnings. It was only a matter of time before it happened. In my mind, the sooner

1

the better. I graduated in 1989 with multiple business degrees.

For the next five years, I did nothing but further educate myself. Furthered my chances to promote and collect pedigrees that would attract Wall Street. I obtained the CPA, CFP®, CLU®, PFS. You name it, I had it. Professional certificates and licenses showing my expertise in wealth and money. Expertise in advising and managing the wealth of America. Not just traditional wealth…my skills propelled me—at the ripe age of 30—to be among the top money advisors to the extraordinarily rich. The top of the top. My client base was composed of some of the wealthiest families in the country.

Client portfolios of $5 million, $50 million, $100 million and more. A sought after client base. The envy of brokers from New York to Dallas. I did it. I captured it. I became it. I lived it.

Advising close to $1 billion in assets of America's wealthy, I was at the top of my game. I was at the top of Wall Street. A seven figure salary. Perks. Big bonuses. Beautiful family. Nice neighborhood. The house. The second home. Nice cars. Fancy boats. Fine jewelry. Luxury vacations. $1,000 a night hotel rooms. $500 bottles of wine. I went from making nothing…to having everything. The American dream.

I was in control. I was handling my life. My affairs. My future. I had the pulse of what mattered and where I needed to be. Go after it. Consume it. Overcome it. Control what you can control. Never let go. Never look back. Never back down. I got us here. I will remain here. Based on me. My actions. My attitude. Myself.

Me. Me. Me.

I wanted what was best for my family, but my balance sheet dictated my actions. The debt, the spending, the consumption, the pursuit of all that this life could provide had me focused on what would benefit me. I had goals to reach. I had to be greedy. I had to have a job—a way of life—that was greedy. And my greed fueled itself.

My work was geared toward that goal. How much could I make? What could I do to make more? My goal was a large earthly portfolio. A bucket of money that would support me and produce happiness. The problem was that I was miserable along the way. I was not fulfilled. I had to change.

I worked a lot and made a lot. Seven figures. Spent most of it, saved some of it, gave very little of it to those who really needed it. My time was focused on my success, accomplishing the American dream.

And I told myself that my success was my family's success. Not that I didn't make time for my wife and kids, they meant the world to me, but I had no clue what they really needed. I was too busy providing a lifestyle.

Anguish. Stress. Emptiness. Longing.

Disheartened. Disillusioned. Bitter. Empty.

Who was in control? Money? Fortune? Me?

Financially secure. Emotionally bankrupt. Spiritually uncertain.

Faith? I had faith. Faith that tomorrow would come. Faith in my abilities. Faith that I could continue this path to continued wealth, fame and fortune. I went to church. I believed. I knew He was out there. I just didn't know how to fit Him into my world. My life. My path. My wealth. My stuff.

Faith was something I did.

Just another appointment on my calendar. Another chance to meet people. My wife believed in worship. Sunday school was needed for our kids. The kids needed to know Him. The kids needed to understand. I knew He was there, yet on my terms.

I believed. Just not now. No time. No change. No acceptance.

No reason. No relation to Wall Street. Nowhere to turn. I had to buckle down. Push ahead. Continue the dream. Regardless of how much I suffered.

Safety and Security of My Office

My office became my comfort zone. For me and my clients. My office became a shelter of sorts, further isolating me and my wealth from the real world. Further isolating my clients from the outside. From others. From those who might take it, or try to get some of it. My office turned into a counseling office—for those truly blessed people, financially and emotionally—to allow me to further educate and teach them how we could make more and spend more.

The more successful I became, the more isolated I felt. The more money that poured in, the more scared I became. The more I surrounded myself with the goals and objectives that I had set for myself and our family, the more frightened I became of losing it. My office turned against me. It became a reminder of what I had become and how I had placed myself in a spiraling cycle of need. My office went from a welcome shelter of success, to a never ending nightmare of expectations. Expectations of my family. My employer. My clients. More, not less. Rich, not poor. Success, not failure.

From the bottom, it looked promising. From the top, it looked horrible.

My office became a hiding place. My professional life had become what I wanted. Driven, motivated by the pleasures of this world. I had it. I captured it. Now I had to keep it.

I guess that's where it became a reality. That moment when I realized that having "made it," I had put myself in a mode where I had to continue. I could not turn back. I could not go in a different direction. This was what I chose…or was it?

I will never forget a conversation with a client, as we treaded through a difficult time in the stock markets. We were discussing her portfolio of approximately $10 million, which had recently declined by about $2 million. As we were discussing her situation, I addressed her spending. I suggested cutting back…only to be met with..."at these portfolio levels….I'm feeling the pinch." With over $10 million in the bank, my client, whom I advise, suggests to me that she is pinched, starting to feel uncomfortable about her chances to continue her current lifestyle.

Before, I would brush it off. I would hunker down and guide

and ease her concerns that I could make it back. That we would give her back her wealth…her peace of mind. Strategies that would bring her comfort, make her whole again, get her back to her measure of worth…the $12 million.

Where had I gone wrong? Where had I determined that comfort came from a certain level of wealth? That peace of mind came from a certain level of assets? What had I said, in the past, which pointed these well meaning clients in a direction of measuring their worth, comfort and well-being in a portfolio of cash?

The issue was not the $2 million lost. The issue was that she had $10 million. The issue was that our wealth, our view of safety, rests in our material possessions, rather than a faith in our future. Her views focused on what she had lost, versus what she had. Our views rested with what we could not do, what we could not spend, what we could not consume, now that we have less money.

Was it me? Did I attract and retain clients due to my expertise, or due to my own goals and desires in life? Did I "love" money so much that it became an idol? My life exemplified that fact. As I made it…I bought it. I exploited it. I became it. I collected. I hoarded. I built an empire. Greed was good.

Unfortunately, what I found was a continued desire for something else. An empty feeling in my gut. The more I had, the more I felt we needed. The less I had, the more I knew I needed. Quite a scary feeling.

How did I know I was the problem, rather than the solution? My clients were telling me all along. They were the key. They were telling me what I needed to hear, I just didn't listen.

I have a unique opportunity to engage my clients to shift their focus on what is important. Rather than further fueling their desires for more wealth, isolation and emptiness, I need to assist them in truly appreciating their blessings, and how those blessings can change the world.

But you can't give away something you don't have.

Doing the Research

I consume research. I throw myself fully at a project to make sure I understand it. I use that research to make decisions. I create opportunity. I produce results. The problem this time was that the research would change my world completely. Or at least my world up to that point. What project did I take on? What research report, what book did I devour?

The Bible. The New Testament. The Gospels. Acts. I was in trouble. I knew it.

I read it. I took notes. I bought study guides. I consulted novels. I re-read passages. I went to the internet. I moved from the Bible to the likes of C.S. Lewis, Philip Yancey, Dallas Willard, Rob Bell, David Kinnaman. I self studied. I replaced business books with religious books. My library evolved from "How to Build Your Wealth" type books to "Lead Like Jesus"[2] books.

As I studied, as I researched, I realized that after having this new body of information, I could not turn back. I could not turn away. I could not take this effort and simply place it on a shelf for later. I could not file it away for another time, or another point in my career.

It sat there. In my heart. In my soul. In my thoughts. In my journals and notes. It was an investment I had to make. An investment in myself. An investment for my family. An investment for my clients. An investment for others.

I had read the Bible, and I knew I could not turn my back on what I read. I knew that simple gifts of charity were not sufficient. I needed to experience the pain of the world first hand.

I'm not sure at what low point I decided to take the Juarez trip, but I had to be convinced. I had to be coaxed into doing it. I had to be shoved onto the plane. While my heart was changing, this still seemed extreme. Crazy. Silly. Unwarranted. Stupid.

If you were in my shoes at the time would you want to go? I had spent the previous 20 years determined to distance myself from this class of people. I had labored in the trenches of Wall Street to have success and money to enable me to avoid them altogether.

I locked my door. I had security systems on all my possessions. I stayed on my side of the tracks. I had all the conveniences of this world. I could buy protection and pleasures. I wore $1,000 suits. I owned $10,000 watches. My idea of time off was a second home. My goal of charity was writing a check, placing it in the mail and hoping it got where it needed to be.

The ironic thing about the Juarez trip was that my passport had never been used before. My wife and I had decided several months before that we needed passports for the whole family. Our thoughts were to travel abroad. See the world. Greece.

Rome. Paris. You name it. Spend. Consume. Museums. Hotels. Limos. All the luxury that money could buy.

Instead, my passport's first experience would be to escort me across the border of Mexico into Juarez, in a 16 passenger van. Not Cancun. Not Los Cabos. Not the Baja Peninsula...but Juarez. I knew what I was getting into, and I still went. I had a colleague who does a lot of business in Mexico, and when discovering that I was going to Juarez...all he could muster up for me after the shock wore off was..."Be careful and keep your passport on you at all times." Juarez, a city where the U.S. government routinely warns citizens for travel.

I was heading there...on purpose...in a van. No escorts. No protection. At my direction. For some reason. Searching. Looking for something. Scared to death. Scared of not returning. Scared of those people. What I might encounter. What might happen. Of what I might find.

> **Greedy for something that satisfies.**
>
> **Greedy for God.**

And I went because I was greedy. But it was different now. I was *greedy for God*. I was greedy for something that truly satisfied. I was greedy for something that was no longer about me, greedy for something greater than myself.

> "Perhaps all along, my deepest joy has never been to have all my dreams come true, but rather to have God's one dream come true: that this world will become a place God is at home in, a place God takes pride and pleasure in, a place where God's dreams come true."[3]

2

Discover Your Spiritual Portfolio

LESSON: Focus On Your ~~Net~~ ^Self^ Worth

Jesus Who?

While Gordon Gekko wasn't necessarily my hero, I certainly wanted to be a part of the world he inhabited. And then suddenly, I find myself there and I still feel empty.

And like I've always done, I do a little research, start perusing the pages of God's Word for something that will fill me up and I don't have to search far, because the kind of life I've always been searching for—long before I was even seduced by the life of Wall Street—is laid down right in front of me.

But let's lay that aside for a moment, and wonder if perhaps

He had taken a different path.

What if Jesus chose a life outside of service? He had talent. He had skill. He influenced people. He could have ignored those less fortunate. What if He embraced the wealthy, the owners, the kings, the rich? Chose the nice neighborhood. Nice towns. Uptown. The right side of the tracks. Ignored His destiny.

Picture this.

What if Jesus chose wealth, power, money, status? His time was too important for others. What if He focused only on... Himself. Selfish acts. Personal gain. Finger pointing. Blaming others. Exploited those around Him. Made a living. Collected all sorts of things.

Thousands went hungry. The lame, remained lame. The sick, died. The dead, buried. The outcast, squashed, ignored. What if He chose not to be remembered? What would His legacy be? What if He did not serve? Would we remember Him?

I think not. Those first in line are often forgotten. Those last in line stand out. We would have to research Him. We would have to Google Him. He would be hard to find, hidden in the back of some textbook. If He chose a different path, He would have been forgotten. He would have been an after thought.

He didn't. He chose a life of service, mission.

> "[Jesus] who, being in very nature God, did not consider equality with God something to be used to His own advantage; rather, He made himself nothing."[4]

Jesus gave Himself, gave His heart, gave His soul, helped others. He changed those around Him. He healed those in need. He was sinless.

Ensuring Your Legacy

God is asking that you be remembered. Be remembered by those you helped. By those you provided for. By those around you. God will remember. Jesus will remember. Don't worry whether you'll have your name on a building, a room, a wing in Heaven. Ensure your legacy on earth is service, is giving, is mission and your legacy will be remembered in Heaven.

The best gift you can leave behind to those around you is a memory of your selfless attitude to others. As Jesus did. As you remember He did. As those will remember you, on earth and in Heaven.

Jesus is remembered by His service. Intense passion for others. He enjoyed them. Empathized, not sympathized. Their needs, their concerns, their souls. But He didn't serve to be remembered, He served because that was the Will of His Father.

We will be remembered by what we do for others, not ourselves. By our service, our mission.

Remembered by our children. Our parents. Our neighbors. By our good acts. Our good deeds.

But that's a benefit, not the purpose.

We serve because that is the Will of our Father.

Close your eyes. Imagine this.

Judgment Day. You might call it Assessment Day. Appraisal Day. Evaluation Day. It's your turn. You're in line. Hopeful. Heaven is not earned through actions. Grace took care of that. You stand ready for God's evaluation of your use of the treasures He provided during life. Perhaps He will say…"Well done, good and faithful servant!"[5]

Or will He say…"Your Earthly Investment Portfolio is impressive. But why did you leave so much wealth and possessions behind? Those treasures belong to Our Kingdom. Who's caring for it now? Will your loved ones left behind tithe and give? Or will they follow your actions and hoard the blessings I bestowed upon them? I wanted so much more for you. I love you, but your Earthly Portfolio means nothing."

Now open your eyes.

Look around.

Reexamine. Refocus.

God is pleased with our efforts, our spiritual life, our Earthly Portfolio. He asked for more. More devotion. More service. More vision.

Vision is the key. The key to change. To change our focus. As our vision changes, we deposit. God records. God collects. God sees. He sees faith. Faith in action, memory retained.

We cannot earn our way into Heaven. Our actions indicate where our true heart lies. Life is not measured by what we own. God places treasures in the hands of those who will make "God Use" of it. We spend quite a bit of time thinking about retirement. Countless hours managing, studying, reviewing, focusing on our investment portfolios. Hoping, one day, to reap the benefit of a better life. A life without work, worry, doubt. Simply put…the good life.

Yet we yearn for more. More to this earthly life. More than a large bank balance. Money, possessions, wealth, can come with a price. They can leave you empty. Can there be both? Financial security *and* Spiritual Wealth?

As a Financial Advisor, my hope is that my clients have a certain comfort with the direction of their portfolio. A comfort with whether or not it will meet their goals, their vision. A vision of where their wealth is heading, and how they get there. A comfort that they

> **God places treasures in the hands of those who will make "God Use" of it.**

have the right asset allocation, or collection of deposits for the road ahead. Sufficient deposits to get them there. A security that the deposits they place in their portfolio will be broad and diverse to weather any financial crisis, and will produce sufficient assets for the future.

These meetings often include discussions of their legacy and what they expect to leave behind. What legacy goals do my clients have? Will they leave behind a legacy of spending, or collecting? Will they leave behind a legacy of service?

God asks us to focus on His portfolio, His record of our lifetime mission to His Kingdom. Spend a fraction of the time on your Spiritual Portfolio that you spend on your Earthly Portfolio, and rejoice in your wealth in Heaven.

Deposits to the Kingdom

How do we focus on our Spiritual Portfolio? How do we make deposits? What earnings will God provide?

We tithe. We give. We perform good deeds. We serve. We mission. We focus on the needs around us. Those near and dear to our hearts. We are blessed with this account. God has kept an accurate account of our deeds to date. Recognize His blessing of wealth. Focus on building your Spiritual Portfolio. You've had it since birth.

God's keeping track of this portfolio. Our Spiritual Portfolio. God's Spiritual Portfolio is held for us to spend and enjoy during our eternal life. Our life in Heaven and on God's New Earth.

> "Sell your possessions and give to the poor. Provide purses for yourselves that will not wear out, a treasure in Heaven that will not be exhausted, where no thief comes near and no moth destroys. For where your treasure is, there your heart will be also."[6]

Yes, God opened an account in Heaven for us. What does it look like now that you discovered it? What will you deposit to your Spiritual Portfolio? If we knew we had it, we would have focused on it, right? Treat it like a winning lottery ticket you found out about, years after buying your ticket. We focus on our Earthly Portfolios, at the expense of our Spiritual Portfolios.

Now that you have it, fill it.

Fill it with gracious actions:

Deeds, Service, Gifts and Tithes.

You know God. He watches. He monitors. He retains. He reviews our Spiritual Portfolio frequently. We should nurture it, add to it, focus on it, build it, maintain it, pray about it.

Our Spiritual Portfolio reflects how we choose to live. How we choose to behave. How we choose to invest our wealth, our time on earth. A choice. Ourselves or others.

Daily choices.

Weekly choices.

Lifelong choices.

Our Spiritual Portfolios will not save us. We are saved by grace through faith in Jesus.[7] Unearned. Undeserved.

Strive to live as Jesus did. Imitate Christ. Develop, nurture, deposit to the Kingdom. Deposit to your Spiritual Portfolio.

Transform lives. Our life. Today. Tomorrow. Eternally.

Our Spiritual Portfolio is not earned by our actions. Our Spiritual Portfolio is a gift from God. Gifts of financial resources. Gifts of time. Time invested in service. In mission. All gifts from God.

Recognize these gracious gifts.

Refocus our earthly life on Spiritual deposits. Fulfilled life, faithful heart. Eternal life in return for our deposits.

Reinvest what God invested in us. Our blessings. Our faith. Our Holy Spirit. Return those investments to Him. Make deposits. Yearn. Reach.

Perhaps you think your Spiritual Portfolio has a zero balance. Will God recognize deeds and service from the past? Gifts? Tithes? Charity? He has. There were faithful actions you were already doing. Rest assured, it is never too late to start. Begin to deposit. Begin to build your Spiritual Portfolio. God is grace and mercy. Begin late in life, early in life, any moment. God expects once you take on Jesus, you fund your Spiritual Portfolio.

Perhaps others have quite a large and diversified portfolio balance. You've deposited to God's Kingdom. You're tithing, giving, serving. It's stored in Heaven. Those treasures in Heaven you've read about.[8] To whom much is given, much is expected.[9] God doesn't require a certain balance. Certain size. Certain allocation of deposits. God expects more from those who have more. God also expects gifts of time. Our deeds, service and mission work. Time invested to bless the Kingdom. Deposits of our blessings.

Planning for eternity requires a significant amount of time, right?

Wrong.

With God's everlasting grace and mercy, our Spiritual Portfolio can be kick started immediately. Our returns reflect our priorities. Our soul.

Traditional retirement planning targets age 65, or sooner. Remaining life expectancy being 20 more years. We tend to forecast our portfolio balance to ensure sufficient capital for our remaining *earthly* life expectancy. What about our eternal life expectancy? We expect an unlimited number of years, right? We'd better start depositing!

How does one plan for an infinite number of years? That's quite a long life span. Ensure your portfolio is properly diversified, maintained and funded. Does it matter to you now? Will it matter? How about those currently retired?

According to a study by the American Association of Retired Persons (AARP), three-quarters of us ages 50 and over believe in life after death.[10] It does matter. We believe it matters. Faith matters. Works matter. Gifts matter. Charity matters.

Will retirement focus your deposits on service and deeds? Time well invested. Invested in the Kingdom. God is not asking that you cease planning for your retirement. Simply recognize His account set aside for you, and parallel plan for eternity.

That's hard to do! Our entire lives we've been focusing on how we might set aside enough money to ensure our place in the sun, our golden rainbow of retirement. Our goal has been to retire, retire, retire.

Our planning focus needs to change. Until we plan differently, we'll remain fixated on our Earthly Portfolio. We can focus on our Earthly Portfolio, but never at the expense of our Spiritual Portfolio. Our planning for the future will change once we recognize that:

We don't have to know the future to have faith in God, we have to have faith in God to be secure about our future.

Our faith while here on earth assures us that our future is certain.

With this certainty in mind, we should deposit. Deposit because we are *already* forgiven, not to earn forgiveness.

The U.S. Census Bureau[11] indicates baby boomers in this country are at retirement's doorsteps. By the year 2010, approximately 40 million people will be age 65 or older. According to projections, by 2025, 63 million people will be age 65 or older. This comprises 17.9% of the U.S. population.[12] Pre-retirees are focused on their Earthly Portfolio, and remaining earthly life expectancy.

Imagine the impact. The impact as we focus on our Spiritual Portfolio. Imagine the good deeds, service projects, mission work, tithes and charitable gifts. Imagine the impact on God's Kingdom. Those around you. Those hurting. Those in need.

Actuarial research[13] further shows we are living much longer than before. A male age 65 has a 25% chance of living beyond age 92. A female has a 25% chance of living beyond age 94, while a couple has a 25% chance of one of them living beyond age 97.

Imagine, 40 million people focused on their Spiritual Portfolio for another 30 years. That's an astounding 1.2 billion total years of deposits to God's collective "retirement community" portfolios. Better yet, that's 10,950 days for deeds, service, gifts and tithes, or collectively 438 billion days for service to God!

The impact of these collective deposits will have a profound impact on others.

On our world.

On our faith.

On God's Kingdom.

Believe in God? Want to please Him? Want to see what He sees?

We should shift our focus to our Spiritual Portfolio.

Let's begin.

We'll examine the four major components to the Spiritual Portfolio: Deeds, Service, Gifts and Tithes. As our goals with each deposit change, our life, heart, finances and soul change. We'll delve deep into each deposit, ensuring an understanding of the significance of each. Its relation to God's Kingdom and purpose.

Our Spiritual Portfolio has two deposit sources: our Calendar and our Checkbook. Deeds and Service from our Spiritual Calendar, and Gifts and Tithes from our Spiritual Checkbook.

We'll review the sources of deposits, their biblical nature, the earnings God's Kingdom reaps, the diversity of our deposits, the reflection on these deposits, all of which point to our lifelong reward. Our eternal reward.

What condition is your Spiritual Portfolio?

Will the complexion change over time?

How's your eyesight?

Need a new prescription?

Need a pair of Spiritual glasses?

What do God's eyes see?

What has He seen?

What will He see?

Will God retain or discard His vision? His witness to your acts, gifts, service. Wipe away sin or record deeds?

In many ways, we are like the apostle Paul. On the road to Damascus.[14] We're blind. We can't see. Just as Paul was.

Blinded by our ignorance. Our poor intentions. Our control.

Blinded by our indifference. Our choices. Our decisions.

Unable to see light. THE light. Focused on darkness. Focused on earthly things. Focused on our net worth instead of our *self worth*. God is there. We've chosen to close our eyes. Or are they wide open, and we're still blindly stumbling in the dark?

We have a choice. To see what God sees. We need our sight back. As Paul did. Clean lenses. Better prescription. Bright headlamp. Let's find the light.

Welcome to your newly discovered Spiritual Portfolio!

3

God's Calendar: Invest Time or Spend Time

LESSON: Time ^ is Money
for God

A Glimpse of God's Heart

Our best definition of God? Jesus.

A glimpse of God's heart is depicted in the life of Jesus, and reflected in the gospels.

Jesus' love for others. His compassion for others. Jesus embodies how God views those He loves. Jesus is our closest example of what it would be like to be around God. Loving, nurturing, looking beyond your faults, seeing beyond your failures, seeing you how God sees you.

Marcus Borg said it best: "Jesus is, for us as Christians, the decisive revelation of what a life full of God looks like."[15]

Borg crystallized for me what it means to be a Christian. Bluntly indicating as a Christian we are to do two things: love God, and love others. Recreating Jesus in my mind, Borg will recreate Jesus in yours.

We live a life of choices. A choice to change. A choice to retain. A choice to look around. A choice to see life.

Will we spend our time, or will we invest our time? Our time for God's Kingdom. How did Jesus invest? How did Jesus live?

Jesus served. Served the Kingdom. Served thousands. Served His 12 disciples. Served God. Jesus taught while He served. Taught by His actions. Led by example.

Our actions are witnessed. Witnessed by God. Witnessed by Jesus. Witnessed by those around us.

Our Good Deeds show kindness. Service attitude. Recognized. Registered. Recorded.

Service. Servant.

Those words. Variations on the same. Included in the Bible over 900 times. Second only to love. Think it mattered?

Absolutely.

Our actions reap rewards. Reap rewards in Heaven. Return on investment that we will keep for eternity.

God offers dividends. Now. Later.

Our return today? Joyful hearts. Kind hearts. Motivated hearts. Security. Peace.

Tomorrow? Insurance for the afterlife.

To truly follow Christ. To take Him in. To encompass His Holy Spirit? Live like Him. In all you do. In all your actions. He mandates it. He motivates it. He wants it. He records it. Now. Later. Later in your Spiritual Portfolio.

To love others, we must truly love Jesus. Unconditional love of Jesus. Passionate love of Him. To love others, we must feel this in our hearts. Love cannot be faked. Love for Jesus cannot be faked. To truly embrace what Jesus did, we must love Him with all of our hearts.

As God did. As the 12 did. As Paul did. The kind of love that is not pressed, not forced, not shallow. Love seeps from our hearts. To others. Deeds are all about love. Love smiles.

> "Trust pours first from loving hearts committed to serve and support one another, through promises kept, to encouragement and appreciation expressed, through support and acceptance, to repentance and apologies

accepted, to reconciliation and restoration."[16]

If we focus on what God loves, His images on earth, our relationship with God strengthens now, on earth and later in Heaven. We live richer, fuller, loving lives on earth. We love God even more, the more we experience those who *He* loves.

Faithful Deposits. Faithful Service. Permanently Recorded.

The FBI can erase your memory. Or so my son says. He's been watching too much TV or too many sci-fi movies. One cannot erase memory. I've told him time and time again that once you see something…you cannot *unSee* it.

If you see it, it's there, part of your brain's permanent record of life.

Or is it?

Those around us. Suffering. Poverty. In need.

How many times, in the past, have you driven by a homeless man at a red light, with his hand out, and drove on without a moment's thought? As though he wasn't there. Immediately, we push him out of our vision. We choose to ignore it. We ignore that urge to give.

Jesus had choices. A choice to die, a choice to live, a choice to embrace His time on earth. Invest His time on earth. How did He choose?

Humble service. Service to others. Service to the Lord. His Father. Service to the outcast. To the downtrodden. To the expelled. Sick. Lame. Criminal. The lowest levels of society.

Last in line in this world, first in the next.

Jesus was famous for His faithful action. His choices. We're lucky. He liked people.

So should you. Beginning to end. Love of others. Not for our sake, for their sake. Unconditional. We need that feeling. We can have that feeling. We must look around. We must see through God's eyes. Only if you see through God's eyes will it remain.

In this sense, once you see it, you cannot *unSee* it. You cannot erase that memory. You will be reminded as you serve again, what you saw during that service or mission experience.

Deposit.

We must change our memory.

When we serve, we deposit to God's Kingdom. By shifting our focus, we see the world. Once we see it through God's eyes, it is unerased memory.

Permanently recorded. Faithful deposits. Faithful service. We see those in need, in need of our deeds and service, in need of our deposits. Deposits to our Spiritual Portfolio. Deposits to His Kingdom.

Why should we attempt to see the world around us? See those in need?

Who cares?

Who will benefit?

We will. God's Kingdom will. God sees. He sees everything. He's watching. He has eyes. He's set aside a tracking method for your works. Your faith. Your thoughts, intentions, soul.

Let's open our eyes to see.

The first half of your Spiritual Portfolio is all about vision: Good Deeds and Big Deeds. Service and Mission.

How much should we deposit? What ratios of each should we focus on? God simply wants deposits. God's barometer rests with His knowledge of our hearts. Our souls. Our intentions. God wants our lives centered on Jesus. How He lived on earth. How He gave time. Effort. Mission. Himself. He's indifferent.

God wants our focus, our faithful action and faithful service.

In order to give, give with our hearts, we must embrace those around us. Embrace those in need. Those who Jesus focused on. How do we begin to change our perspective? Our vision?

> **Devote time to the Kingdom. Invest your time on earth. Don't simply spend it.**

Devote time to the Kingdom. Invest your time on earth. Don't simply spend it.

Our deposits are all about others. As Jesus' life and attitude was 100% about others. Other people's gains were Jesus' reward. "It's not about me." Jesus deflected attention from Himself.

Our deposits show that we recognize the need to help one another. Deposits that reflect our hearts, and deflect attention away from ourselves.

God watches as we deflect.

Seek to deflect attention to others, for a more fulfilled life.

Deposits are habitual. Developed habits. God wants them. Simple habits. Second nature. Stop thinking about them. Just do them. The more we deposit, the more they become us. Our soul.

Our legacy. God wants our habits focused on His Kingdom. His rewards.

Those around us should expect it, not marvel at it. Our efforts should be a part of us, what we are known for.

Jesus was normal. He treated His service as normal. He treated Bartimaeus that way. Blind Bart was normal. Jesus' attitude towards him was love, service, compassion, normalcy. Jesus sensed his faith, his desire to see the light, to see again, to embrace his Father in God through Jesus. For Jesus, normal course of business.

"What do you want Me to do for you?"[17] was His question to Bart. Not for Bart to bow down. Not for Bart to kiss His ring. Not for Bart to pray. Not for Bart to get on His calendar or His agenda. Not for Bart to step aside. Rather to Bart He asked, "What do you want Me to do for you?"

For Jesus, He knew before He ever asked. "Go," said Jesus, "your faith has healed you."[18]

Bart was changed forever, his sight restored, his faith strengthened. Jesus' habits became what He was. What He was remembered by.

Our deposit habits become what we are remembered by.

Our deposits are inclusive, not exclusive. Deeds *include* those who are typically excluded. Mission is about including those who are poor, in pain; a reversal from their life of exclusion.

Jesus included. So should we. He fellowshipped with the outcast, the downtrodden, the tax collectors. He embraced the lame, sick, lepers.

So should we. Our deposits include those around us as part of God's Kingdom.

Jesus makes us want to imitate Him. He challenges us to reconsider who we hang out with on earth. Jesus hung out with peasants—the poor—in villages. He avoided cities. He lived across the tracks, the wrong side of town, where those in need lived. He invites us to visit, embrace, give and serve. As He did.

Our entire deposit portfolio is centered around this request. His request to visit and see what He has seen. "Blessed are the poor in spirit, for theirs is the Kingdom of Heaven."[19]

Deeds start with love. Love in all fashions. Love of all things. Especially others. Those around you. Those far from you. Those images. Images of God. Other images. We are all images. Images of Him.

To love others, we must realize in God's eyes, we are all the same. Same image. Same love. Love He has for all of us.

Paul said it best: "Love is patient, love is kind. It does not envy, it does not boast, it is not proud. It is not rude, it is not self-seeking, it is not easily angered, it keeps no record of wrongs. Love does not delight in evil but rejoices with the truth. It always protects, always trusts, always hopes, always perseveres."[20]

Let me guess, no time to serve. You want the easy way out. Too busy to serve in any meaningful manner.

Not true. The busiest people often serve the most. Busy schedules, yes. But they make it fit. Plan your Big Deeds. Mark your calendar. Set your goal to serve.

Our family goal is three to five vacation days each year for service. We devote time to serve. Delivering meals to those in need (four hours per month). Build houses for the poor (one Saturday per month). Set goals at home. Involve your family. Involve your children. Your neighbors are doing it. They serve. Add yourself to the list.

Proof? About 61.2 million people volunteered through or for an organization at least once between September 2005 and September 2006, the Bureau of Labor Statistics of the U.S.

Department of Labor reports. That's 26.7% of our population.[21] Were you one of them? God recognized these 60+ million service account deposits.

According to the study, those volunteers served on average 52 hours per year (an hour a week, four hours per month, or six plus days per year). Men and women. Men invested about 52 hours, while women reported 50. Some volunteers reported a high of 104 hours in any given year![22] Where did these missionaries invest their time? Religious organizations (35% of all volunteers), followed by educational/youth service related (26.4%), and 12.7% for social or community service organizations.[23]

Worn Out. Sweaty. Dirty Jeans.

Back to my son. I had had enough. No more TV. No more FBI stories. I needed proof. He needed proof. Proof for him. Proof that his memory could be changed. Proof that his memory would be retained. Proof that he could see something and be changed for life. Or at least a period of time.

My son asked one Saturday where I was heading. Where was I going for the entire day without him? Without his sister. To work? To shop? To play golf? What was it?

Better yet, when I returned, more questions. I looked battered and bruised. Worn out. Sweaty. Dirty jeans. White T-shirt completely filthy. Mangled hair. Various scrapes and cuts on my forearms. Must have been a fight? Must have had to change a tire? Better yet, completely rework the engine to get home?

No. I had spent the day with a group of people building a home[24]. A needed home. A home for a family. A needy family. A great group of other caring individuals with no business building homes. Hammering nails, hanging sheetrock, roofing, painting. But we did.

My Saturday was one of various Saturdays spent building the home. All walks of life, all ages, all shapes and sizes, one mission. To extend a hand. Extend care. Strangers caring for strangers. Yet strangely enough, we began as strangers, but ended as comrades.

Funny how a recognition of what you don't know or can't do, humbles you. I have a desk job. I don't hammer nails for a living. My nails are crooked, at best. I take a couple dozen strikes per nail. I became better at pulling crooked ones out, than getting them in. No matter, no worries. We were all in the same boat. There are experts, thank heavens, who show us what to do.

Where to stand. What to hammer. What not to do.

The result is important. The action, just as important. The act of helping. Serving. Spreading faith. Performing deeds. Making deposits.

My son wasn't satisfied with my attempts to describe the process, the charity, the purpose. He wanted to witness it. His own eyes. His own opinion. So he tagged along on dedication day. A half a day where minor (yeah, right) tasks are performed to ready the home for the new homeowner. A chance to do a little work, see a little faith in action and permanently engrain a setting in his eyes.

What happened? My memory changed. My sight refocused. My heart tugged. Again.

Not his. His is fine. Untarnished, to a point, at age 13. He still sees the world as God sees it.

We worked hard, planted grass, shrubs, trees, flower beds. We cleaned the backyard, finished trim painting, set locks, sweated. Dedication time. Announcements. Welcome to the home. Present the keys. Workers in the front yard. Homeowners on the porch.

First home. First set of keys. First chance to cross the

threshold. Tears, joy, laughter. Family. Newly created family. Extended family. The homeowners. The workers.

One big happy family.

What did I see? My vision? My son in front. Too close.

Not in the back with me. Not standing where I unconsciously decided to stand. In the back. Unassuming. Humble. Witnessing the dedication. Hearing the words spoken. Seeing the joy and tears. All from afar.

He was front and center. Practically on the front porch, their front porch. The house was dedicated, it was theirs now, and my son? Bingo. Exchanging breath. Breathing on them.

He wanted to see it. He wanted to see the beauty and joy of what he had just accomplished.

He was proud of it. The homeowners were proud of it. I realized the homeowners wanted him there. Wanted me there. Wanted us there. They wanted us nearby, not far away. Not standing in the back.

God wants my son's attitude in each one of us. He wants us front and center. Experiencing those in need. Close enough to exchange breath. Witnessing their life, assisting their life, depositing for their life…and our eternal life.

We (mostly me) collected our tired bones and jumped in our car.

Heading home. First minute or so, silence. That silence where each one of us collects our thoughts, recalls our morning, remembers the dedication. The joy, the peace, the contentment. No words, just gazing ahead.

My son broke the silence. Finally. Beautifully.

"Dad…can we do that again?"

With tears forming, slowly turning, I replied "Sure."

Compassion. Lives changed. Reasons to serve, reasons to give.

Service is multidimensional. Not only do we serve to this day, we also give to this day. We give knowing other families are in need. We give due to our memory of that Saturday. Those Saturdays. We give because our family knows how important financial gifts are to those memories we create in God's eyes. To those lives we change.

Why should we serve?

Serve not because you think it is the right thing to do, rather do it because you are forgiven and you are looking forward to rewards in Heaven. "It is what we do with our lives. Our righteous works will follow us to Heaven."[25]

And what better time than now.

God's Calendar

January. Renew. Refresh. Begin. Set Goals. Envision the year ahead.

New Calendar. Empty Calendar.

Do you enjoy new calendars?

I do. Fresh start.

What do you do with your new calendar?

I mark it up. I fill it in. I fill it with birthdays, anniversaries, weddings, graduations, holidays, vacations. You name it. I fill it with memorable days and events surrounding those who I love. Those who I care about. Days or events that I want those around me to realize that I'm thinking about them. That I care. If I tried hard enough, I might have an action item for someone on about 60 to 90 of those 365 days.

What about God's calendar?

Imagine that.

What must He have to place on His calendar? What must He have to remind Himself of throughout the year?

He knows my birthday. He knows my anniversary. He knows when my children were born. He knows all and it comforts me.

Our earthly calendar should be our record of memories. Our reminder calendar of dates and events that matter most to those we love. To those who matter to us. Our calendar should include those we are taught by Jesus to love. Those around us. Our neighbors, our friends. Those in need. Those far away. Those in pain.

Mark up your calendar with time you expect to spend on those in need. Your service. Your mission to the Kingdom.

We should block out time to spend and time to reflect on our work for God. Our calendars should be filled with time spent on others, not ourselves. Like God's calendar. No time to reflect on Himself. Rather all the millions of children He has. Like Jesus' calendar.

Did Jesus ever sit in January and fill up His calendar with vacation time, time at the spa, TV time, time on holiday?

Of course not. Jesus saw His calendar as your calendar. His calendar focused on others. As our calendar can be. Fill your calendar with memories of service. Of mission. Fill it with the needs of others. As Jesus did. As God does.

Recognizing that *time spent for God is money* in the bank— or in the Spiritual Portfolio, so to speak—let's start on our deeds, our service, our mission. Our time invested on earth. Our Spiritual Calendar. Time devoted to serve God. The Deeds, the Service, the Mission to the Kingdom.

4

Spiritual Deposit: Good Deeds

LESSON: It's All About ~~Me~~ *You*

"Did Jesus smile?" My daughter asked one morning on the way to school.

"Absolutely," I replied. "All the time. Everywhere He went." To everyone He encountered. Shocking to those around Him. He made an impact, an impression. Folks thought He was odd. Weird. He showed us a new way of life.

Happiness in others. Doing good for others. Placing your happiness in others. Their fate. Their feelings. Their care. Their needs. Deposits to the Kingdom.

Seek these feelings. It's fine to seek this feeling. God wants this feeling in us. Seek it. Search for it. Be selfish about it. Selfish about mission. About service. Anticipate the joy you will feel. Yearn for that joy you find, and will find, in loving others. Doing deeds. Reaching out.

It's contagious.

Catch the bug.

Love is a feeling we should seek out. It's measured by God. He looks for it. We should be motivated by it. Seek rewards as it relates to the love we share and provide to others. God motivates us by offering rewards in eternal life. Lasting rewards. Not temporary rewards. Love should be sought out. Love for others should be a habit. Habit forming.

Form your deposit habits.

Jesus wants habits. He wants your passion. Passion for Good Deeds. Passion for deposits.

Motivate yourself. Like you save for retirement, save for eternal life. No debt. Your treasure is in Heaven. His reward for you. You can reach it. He offers it. He shows you in the end. He's proud. You're proud. The faithful actions on earth.

Embrace it. Enjoy it. It's fun.

Smile. Be nice.

Ever try it?

I did. To the extreme. For about five minutes in a Wal-Mart parking lot. I smiled, waved, said hello to everyone I passed. Everyone in sight. My kids witnessed it. It felt great. Some smiled, some frowned, others giggled.

I was weird. It felt good. Others felt good. I know it. He knows it. It's extreme, but it makes you love life. Eventually, my kids asked that I stop.

Focus on Jesus' smile. What does it look like? Look like to you? Perhaps reflected in the smiles of those you serve?

He smiles a lot. He smiled a lot. Envision His smile.

Their smiles. Your deposits of Good Deeds, service to others, smiles. You want smiles.

Get smiles. Get deposits.

A New Way of Living

Good Deeds are unselfish acts toward others. Caring for others as Jesus cared. A new way of life. A new way of living. Faithful actions to those in need. Embrace Jesus' way of life.

Live better. Feel better.

Good Deeds. A random act. A random act of kindness. A reaction to those around us.

Good Deeds respond to an immediate sense of those in need. Acts of kindness in reaction to something we experience.

Good Deeds come by our commitment to kindness. We all have it, compassion for others.

Jesus was the King of compassion.

We are made in His image. Our compassion is there. We must dig for it. Suppressed emotions deep in our hearts. Experiencing others will bring those emotions to the forefront. To the surface.

> **Good Deeds come by our commitment to kindness.**

Changing our attitude. Changing our actions. Changing our lives.

Good Deed deposits require an attitude adjustment.

Jesus asks that we change. Wake up and look around.

"To be this kind of person—the kind who selflessly serves—takes everything a person has. It is difficult. It is demanding. And often we find ourselves going against the flow of those around us."[26]

Good Deeds are caring for others. No matter who they are, where they are. Each and every thought, as it relates to others, could be a Good Deed.

Take an elderly woman by the hand as she walks down a set of stairs. Good Deed.

Deposit.

Jesus wants this again, and often. "This is my command: Love each other."[27]

We could ignore this elderly woman, continue on with our lives, check our BlackBerry®, call someone, look in the other direction, move on. God calls us to notice. To see. To notice those around us, and act.

Where do we start? How do we effortlessly begin these deposits to our Spiritual Portfolio? How do we open our eyes to see life around us? To reflect on the true life we're asked to live on earth?

Begin at home. Simply put, but important. Good Deeds begin here. Open your eyes at home.

Serve your families, for they have eyes. Eyes of our children, our spouses, our parents, our grandparents. Our neighbors. Our community. Those around us witness our actions, how we act toward others. Exhibit compassion. Serve each other.

Husbands, serve your wives. Wives, serve your husbands. Children, serve your parents. Parents, serve your children. Ensure you're there when needed. Show compassion by your actions. Jesus wants us to serve one another, particularly our families.

Does it matter? Does it work? Will your new eyesight rub off on those around you? My daughter is example enough.

Roaming Goblins and Good Deeds Recognized

Halloween night. We've covered two blocks. She approaches yet another door. I notice her bend down to pick up something from the door stoop. Passing it to the homeowner, an exchange of words. My daughter reaches out, receives. Pleasantries exchanged. Deposit.

Come to discover, my daughter, all of nine years old, returned a $20 dollar bill found on the doorstep. The homeowner must have dropped it, or so she thought. Better yet, a roaming goblin could have lost it. It wasn't hers...it must have been someone else's.

Honesty comes naturally, in the beginning. We once had it. It left. We must find it. Search for it. Capture it. Honesty comes to those who witness it in others. Our environment reproduces this action. This Good Deed. Unadulterated kindness. Deposit to her evolving Spiritual Portfolio.

Nice huh? Better yet, her gift was her generosity. $20 in return. From the homeowner. To her. In her pocket.

In His pocket. His memory. A recognition of her Good Deed, just as God does. He recognizes these deeds. Her exuberance shined through. No expectations. Good Deeds go recognized, by God and others.

Good Deeds are contagious. Honesty, Good Deed nature. Perhaps her environment, hopefully her environment.

Once we returned home, she asked for change. Break her $20 into small bills. Her tithe was needed. Her two dollars on Sunday. It's contagious. Witness it. Imagine it. Copy it. Imitate it.

Imitate Christ.

Extend beyond your home. Sunday School teachers serve

your children. Pastors serve your congregation. Employees serve your employer. Employers serve your employees. Tithers serve your church. Churches serve your tithers. Serve as Christ did. Fathers serve your family. Mothers, each other.

Serve, don't judge. Unconditional service. Unconditional deeds. Merciful deeds to others.

Rediscovering Love

Good Deeds reflect not only how we behave and act, but how we speak and deal with others.

Kind words, kind smiles, kind thoughts. Thank you. After you. You go first. Deposits make for a better place to live. Heaven on earth. Today. Now.

Our words, thoughts and actions impact those around us. Those we encounter on a daily basis. Those at the workplace, or home. One never knows who might be hurting, what they may be facing, when they encounter us.

Perhaps those strangers, those who cut in line, cut you off. Pulled out in front of your car. Rudely looked away. Acted dismissive. Perhaps they lost someone special. Were fired earlier from their job. Have a child performing poorly in school. You name it. You will never know.

> "Eternal souls will never be the same because of the things you say and do today. Have you asked Jesus to guide your thoughts and guard your tongue…The next person you meet will be glad you did."[28]

Assist that elderly lady…deposit. Purchase those cookies at the door…deposit. Place a dollar, quarter, hope in that offering plate. Visit that nursing home you pass daily. Call your friend to say "You are a friend." Deposits to His Kingdom.

Actions and deeds are a central part of our lives on earth. Jesus embraced those around Him. So should we.

Grin and Bear It

This all sounds well and good. What if I don't feel like it? After all, visiting a nursing home might be nice, but I don't see how it's going to make much of a difference. Wouldn't my time be better spent handing out Bibles or preaching in some Third World Country?

Sound familiar? Feel familiar?

Think of the 12 Disciples. What did they see? Who did they

encounter? How did they behave? Where did they go? Did they want to? People, places and things you would not want to see, or do. Just like service. Just like mission. Making yourself see life that you don't normally see.

They followed Jesus for His words. They followed Jesus for His teachings. They followed Jesus because. Just because. They followed Jesus for His actions. His faithful actions for the Father, for the mission, for the Kingdom. That's where it started, and that's where the 12 became human in my mind. Human like me. Not characters in a book. Not glorious angels from the Bible. Humans. Humans with emotions. Humans with fears, doubts, questions, complaints.

Images of God. Images of us.

They followed Jesus to places they had avoided in the past. Uncomfortable places. Uncomfortable homes. Odd people. Weird people. Criminals. Homeless. I bet they fussed. I bet they whined. They must have. Read it in the scripture. Mumbling. Complaining. Frowning. Pointing.

What if the scripture included the following: "Where are we going, Jesus? More of the same? How can we feed them? There must be thousands! What difference will it make? More will come, and more problems. Are we going to spend all of our time acting?"

The hungry. Desolate. Blind. Lame.

"Do we have to? I'm busy. We're busy! We've got preaching to do. We've got temples to visit. Should we really be bothered with these vagrants when we have more Godly things to do?"

Sound familiar? Feel familiar?

I bet so. I have those emotions daily. Every time I head out to serve. Every time I head out on a mission trip. Every time I consider donations.

We are human. The 12 were human. Imagine those 12. Imagine those images. Imagine what was not recorded in the Bible. It happened, I know it did. Some of it was written, but not all of it. The gospel writers were kind.

Jesus faced this scrutiny. Jesus faced these challenges. Jesus was tempted, believe me. He was tempted to turn the other direction. Tempted to ignore those in need, those in pain, those suffering.

But Jesus didn't. They kept coming. The lepers. The sick. The unbelieving. Jesus ignored what He should have ignored.

He ignored those feelings He had to turn away. Those feelings to abandon His mission. He ignored those gripes and complaints of his 12.

Instead, He embraced. He embraced those in need. He chose to smile. To smile at Himself. To smirk perhaps. He smiled at His followers, His 12. "…O you of little faith?"[29]

Jesus smiles at us. He smiles when we choose to serve. He smiles when we complain. When we gripe. When we choose to wonder if it matters, if our small little Saturday afternoon serving really makes a difference. He smiles when we recognize the enormous uphill battle we face. Jesus smiles when we attempt to gather our own agenda. When our thoughts take us to better, more comfortable places. When we are anxious encountering those in need. The homeless, the sick, the prisoners.

He smiles because He remembers. Jesus remembers His 12. Same emotions. Same doubts. Same fears. Same anxiety. He knows how we feel. How we feel before we even feel it.

Make Him smile. Make Him credit your account. Credit for your affections to others. Credit for your Good Deed mentality. He motivates. You act. He rewards. You perform. Seek rewards. Seek action. Get out and Deed.

Say *Please*. Wave at your neighbor. Call your sibling. Say *Thank You*. Say *I Miss You*. Give. Open a door. Say *I Love You*. Care. Smile. Visit your parents. Write a Thank You note. Say *Hello* to a stranger. Visit the hospital. Visit a nursing home. Adopt a child. Mentor a child. Hug someone. Send a card. Serve a meal. Love someone. Place a dollar in the plate. Donate a dollar. Prepare a meal. Offer your chair. Defer to someone else. Play with your children. Start at home. Include your spouse. Love your spouse. Read to a child. Love your children. Donate blankets. Donate possessions. Donate clothes. Empathize. Be kind.

Jesus Riding Shotgun

My kids constantly fight over who sits in front.

"I've got shotgun." "NO! I've got shotgun."

Could Jesus ride shotgun? Is Jesus riding shotgun? Who's riding shotgun?

Think about it.

Jesus riding shotgun. With you. While you travel. While you reach stop lights. While you head off to work. On the bus. On the train. In your car.

Would you behave differently?

I would. I do. My deeds increase. My service attitude changes. My Jesus attitude sparkles.

Sitting at a stoplight. Homeless man. With Jesus riding shotgun, I turn to glance at Jesus. Not necessary. I know what to do. Help him out. Provide a few bucks for a meal. With Jesus riding shotgun, no reason to ponder, get out your money.

Imitate Christ. Imitate His passion.

Assist others.

I'm not sure I'd ever get where I'm going if Jesus rode shotgun. Jesus would stop at every corner. He'd ask that I pull over countless times. He'd direct me to locations and places of those in need. I'd be on an endless journey. Finding those in need. Caring for those around us.

In effect, Jesus rides shotgun. Today. Now, more than ever. Jesus rides shotgun with me daily as I embrace deposits to His Kingdom. As Jesus rides shotgun, the world changes. Our outlook changes. Our deposits change.

Try it. It's fun. Include your children. Pretend Jesus is riding shotgun. Leave the passenger seat empty.

I did. My son, daughter and I rode to the mall. Kids in the back, me and Jesus in the front. The chatter was wonderful. The reflection permanent. As we tooled around town, we witnessed Jesus frown as others in our path honked. As others sped past. Cut people off. Obviously no shotgun partner. On other occasions we witnessed kindness, caring, politeness…Jesus must be riding shotgun with those families.

As we played our game of "Find Jesus Riding Shotgun," we noticed we cared for others. We cared for strangers. We made an effort to be kind. To be warm, welcoming. We searched for cars with Jesus riding shotgun.

Our deeds, our service to others, our deposits, reflect whether or not Jesus is riding shotgun. As Jesus jumps in our car, we change. We focus on deposits. We recognize that *it isn't about us*, and we focus on others.

Allow Jesus inside your car. Allow Jesus to ride shotgun. He'll change your focus. He'll change your attitude. He'll change your outlook on life, and how to live it. Jesus riding shotgun.

5

Spiritual Deposit: Big Deeds

LESSON: ~~First~~ *Last* ^ in this World

A Ragtag Group of Hooligans

When it comes to business, it's about doing whatever it takes to make your client happy. Happy Client. Happy Brandon. It's as simple as that. And I've spent the biggest part of my life doing whatever it takes to get what I think I need.

This attitude didn't go away when it came to doing whatever it took to fill my empty space with something spiritual. I was willing to go to any lengths. Only my purpose had changed.

Big Deeds. Well thought out. Planned in advance. Mission and service. To serve or not to serve. I'm writing this section—

or better yet beginning this section—on the eve of a mission trip to Juarez, Mexico.[30] A true mission trip. A bunch of guys getting together to take a three day trip to a remote part of Mexico to build houses for poor families.

I'm lucky, I get a chance to see the other side of the coin. Mission and service to others, our deeds, are all about seeing. Once you see it, it remains.

Get a group. Get a mission team. Group of people. Your 12, or four, or your family. Like Juarez, or Russia, or across the tracks, downtown in your town, around the corner. There are plenty of places to go, to help, to serve.

Like the 12 disciples. In my case, during a recent trip to Juarez, there were 22 of us. Ragtag group of hooligans. Different levels of passion. Walking with Christ…or better yet, driving across the border with Christ…or flying to El Paso first with Christ, then driving across the border with Christ, to Mexico. Groups breed consistency. Groups mean more. More memories.

Me? Sitting in the back of a 16 passenger van, car sick, looking around, trying to focus. Bouncing. Bumping. Where are we? Why are we here?

Pain. Poverty.

Life as God sees it. I'm seeing it. I'm experiencing it.

What if He were here? Jesus here, today. He would recruit. He would retain depositors. What would earth be like if we deposited? All of us, with Jesus here? If Jesus lived and ruled the earth. Now.

Heaven on earth.

What would it mean? Work. Lots of work. If Jesus were here with us, He would be busy. Very busy. Lots to do.

He needs our help, in advance of His return. He wants our deposits so that He can see our progress. He wants our faithful action to know who to recruit to His team.

What if His return was like His last three years on earth, the first time? Who would He see first? Who would He approach?

Depositors.

Not to congratulate. But to empower. Empower us to do more. To continue what we are doing. To continue depositing. He would be right along side us. Cheering. Seeing. Pointing out those in need. Those we missed.

Would Jesus seek out those who are rich and powerful? Those in control? Those with stored up treasures on earth? He would, if they were depositors. Jesus would encourage further deposits. Extend your reach beyond what you had been doing before.

Jesus would also seek those in need, in pain. The suffering. The sick. The depressed. He would use our deposit resources to care. To solve. To embrace. We would be servant depositors for His mission. The Lord's mission.

Jesus would link stored treasures with service attitudes. With compassionate minds. He would link lives of financial resources with lives of service and mission. Empower resources to benefit God's Kingdom.

Pretend He is here. Pretend He's looking over your shoulder. When you give. When you serve. Pretend He's at your house when you return from a soup kitchen. What would He say? What would He utter as you walked through the door?

Perhaps "How did that feel?"

Or "Did they smile?"

Or "Were you welcome there?" "Did you feel love?" "Did you feel pain?"

Or "Were you uncomfortable?"

One thing is for certain, Jesus knows our memory will never

be the same. We are changed from within. Our hearts, our minds, our memory. Internal change.

Back to mission, Juarez perhaps. Our perception is poverty. Their perception, life as is. We see pain, they see normalcy.

Change your perspective. Stop comparing. Service is not about us or how we view their life. It's about caring, helping, reaching out.

Lose our agenda. See beyond ourselves. Love unconditionally. Lose the *me* attitude. Lose the benefit you are searching for. Win the benefit to others. Lose yourself. Others attitude. Other focused. Others in need. The poor. Deposits for others. Love as a brother. Love as a sister. As yourself. Treat as equals. No order. No priority.

Look in the mirror. Look in their mirror. Keep their mirror. Take it from their wall. See their image. Memorize their reflection. See their reflection. Reflect on it. Retain it. What you see is mission. Mission needed.

Equalize yourself. Equal images. Human beings. Different circumstances. Same form of birth. Same form of death. Where will you go? Your eternal life? What do you see? What does He see? See their reflection in God's eyes. You want God looking at you. Fill His eyes with your actions. Your service and mission.

> "It starts with a simple awakening to the suffering around you. It opens you up to a world that is more rich and reflective of the heart of God."[31]

Big Deeds feel big to us. To God they aren't. To God they are routine. Normal.

> **Big Deeds are those we plan in advance. Dedicated time set aside to spread hope to the world.**

Big Deeds are those we plan in advance. Dedicated time set aside to spread hope to the world. Time pre-determined to see something around you. To experience life we don't routinely see.

Our eyesight is our key to the Kingdom. Our key to deposits to our Spiritual Portfolio.

> "Jesus was sent by His Father to the poor to be able to understand the poor. Jesus had to know and experience that poverty in His own body and soul. We too must experience poverty if we want to be true carriers of God's love. To be able to proclaim the Good News to the poor we must know what is poverty."[32] – Mother Teresa

If we see what we know is there (poverty, injustice, suffering), we are compelled to act. Jesus was the King of action. Jesus didn't have a bag of money to donate. He served.

In Luke, Jesus says, "But I am among you as one who serves."[33] As Rob Bell—author of *Velvet Elvis: Repainting the Christian Faith*—puts it, "He not only refers to Himself as a servant, sent to serve others, but He teaches His disciples that the greatest in His Kingdom are the ones who serve."

Bell further states, "The best and greatest and most important are the ones who humble themselves, set their needs and desires aside and selflessly serve others."[34]

Big Deeds share our time. Gifts and Tithes share our possessions. Time is vital. Seeing is vital...to God's Kingdom. Dedicate time—just as you would money—to service and mission. Set goals. Monthly. Yearly. Devote vacation time. Serve in your neighborhood, your town, your city. Go overseas.

Consider your talents and your hobbies when you serve.

Architect, electrician, plumber...build homes.

Chef, server, food critic...deliver meals or serve in a soup kitchen.

Doctor, nurse, caregiver...visit nursing homes. Care for the mentally challenged.

The list is endless. Sightsee with your talents and interests.

Search the needs around you.

The impact is great, measured, deposited.

When you see those in need, what will you find? Those first in line. Those who enter the Kingdom first. "But many who are first will be last, and many who are last will be first."[35]

Where to go? Not far. Begin near your home. Jesus suggests we humble ourselves.

How? Go see. Find those in need. Notice the long line you face at Kingdom's doorstep. Our deposits retain our spot, perhaps move us closer to the front.

Recognized.

As we experience mission and service, you might be surprised. Those in need are fine, OK, content. Is there any other life?

Seeing is believing. Smiles, thanks, appreciation. Your deposits matter. To God. To those in need.

> "It is almost as if being a good missionary means having really good eyesight. Or maybe it means teaching people to use their eyes to see things that have always been there; they just didn't realize it. You see God where others don't. And then you point Him out. Perhaps we ought to replace the word missionary with tour guide, because we cannot show people something we haven't seen."[36]

Service Language

Service to others—love of others—has its own language. A language that is heard and understood by all. A "tongues" of sorts as discussed and described in the Bible. As we deposit, we learn this language, this new language that becomes engrained in our hearts. Our hearts change as we fill it with these signs and symbols.

What language is that?

The language of the eyes, the language of expression. No words spoken, rather a visual in others, and ourselves.

During my first mission trip to Juarez, Mexico, the language barrier was tough. I spoke no Spanish. Not a lick. I took French in high school and college. The chance, or lack of, to visit with those around me was difficult, embarrassing.

As we built homes for the needy, as we imitated Christ in our work, many could speak the language. The conversations seemed wonderful. Full of thanks, excitement, joy. Appreciation for the work being done by our mission group.

For me, all I could do was work. Look around. Wonder what was being said.

Language was all around me. I just missed it. I didn't participate. I didn't focus on it. I was worried about the spoken language, and missed the true language. The language of thanks. Of appreciation. Of grace. Language spoken directly to me. Directly to those around me.

Through their eyes.

The eyes of those in need at the sight of selfless mission teams. Motivated members of Christ traveling to Mexico to build homes for strangers.

As I turned deaf to Spanish, ceased trying to understand the spoken word, I heard the true language of those around me. Their smiles of joy. Their eyes of appreciation. Eyes of peace. Thanks to God.

The more I looked, the more I heard. The more I understood. Language in facial expressions. In heartfelt glances. In Christ-like smiles. I noticed the language of thanks. The language of loving others.

I noticed my language change.

I smiled. I said *thanks*. I had joy.

Rather than constant determination to understand the spoken

word, I let myself speak the new language. I passed on eye contact to those families who truly loved what I was doing. Why we were there. I loved them as images of our Kingdom, as fellow images of God.

Our deposits create a new language. A language of giving, service and mission. A language from our true love of God and love of others. Be it Russian, Spanish, or some other far away language, the language of love and appreciation is spoken universally with our eyes. With our expressions. With our smiles.

"…We should be looking away from ourselves, and at the world we are supposed to be serving."[37] As Jesus did. Jesus served. We should serve.

Begin today. Plan today. Start today. Do not wait. Our eternal time horizon forces us to examine our deposits now. Our Spiritual Portfolio.

Is there sufficient mission work to be done? For sure. Jesus is looking for our gifts of service to His Kingdom. "…the Lord will reward everyone for whatever good he does, whether he is slave or free."[38]

God watches, records, retains our actions. Our intentions. Our Good Deeds. Go Deposit.

Serving in Your Undies

My kids and I signed up for a "Great Day of Service."[39] An entire day devoted to serving missions connected with our church. Our charity of choice supported and cared for children who are victims of abuse and neglect. Closely tied with social services and the local police department, the charity provided— as one of many services—a "store" of sorts for the children.[40]

On many occasions—due to family circumstances of violence, drug use and neglect—children would be removed from their abusive homes and brought to our charity. A safe place. Safe adults. Care in a time of need.

These children are there for a re-birth of sorts, and new life...potentially with other family members or foster homes. In transition, the children need basic items. The "store" held brand new items kids could choose from, having left their troubled homes in a rush on most occasions. Escorted out by social services. Removed by the police due to circumstances out of their control. Literally left their homes with only the clothes on their backs.

Our mission that Saturday was to sort clothes. Donated clothes. Mounds of clothes. Brand new clothes. Donated by the community. Clothes of kindness for their time of transition.

Many of these kids never had new clothes. Never had a chance to pick. To choose. To select. To shop. Clothes. Shoes. Pants. Backpacks. School supplies.

Of all these clothes to sort, what did my kids choose?

Underwear.

Not the shirts, belts, socks, shoes…the underwear. Boy did they have underwear.

A basic need I hadn't focused on. The basic needs many of those kids had. We all have. The need for underwear.

Boys' underwear was our special assignment.

All shapes, all sizes, all colors. You name it. Mounds of donated underwear. Deposited underwear. Underwear for kids in a time of need. We didn't just sort by size (toddler to adult), but within size. We sorted by color (solid or plaid), by type (briefs or boxers), by cartoon character (Pooh or Mickey), by super hero (Batman or Superman), by sports (soccer or baseball), by movies (Toy Story or Finding Nemo)…to name a few.

My kids created an elaborate sorting system other volunteers marveled at. A system of kindness. Selfless emotion and energy for children they didn't know. They simply knew the circumstances. A preparation for children to have a chance to enjoy something. Enjoy the thrill of putting on underwear.

The first thing a child would put on. The first sign of care when these kids enter a new life. A new family. A new situation.

The underwear was a sign of our work.

We sorted underwear for nearly three hours. My kids couldn't have been happier. There's something about underwear that thrilled my kids. Their interest in making sure when those kids shop for clothes, they knew where to turn.

My children embraced their pain. Their emotions. They knew—unlike I did at the time—the kids would enjoy the amazing variety. The choices. It's fun to choose from neat stacks, rather than boxes of clothes. The kids would know we cared. Cared enough to sort the undies.

My kids taught me a lesson. The shoppers taught me a lesson. The need can be basic, as basic as underwear. The need is there.

The children appreciate the sorting. The children appreciate the safe haven. The children appreciate the second chance.

I haven't witnessed the children actually shopping, and

I'm not sure I could take it. Abused, neglected, victims of their surroundings starting over. Having to "shop" for clothes for an undefined period of time, that could mean forever. A change of circumstances. A new encounter. A scene that has played over and over in my mind.

Permanently in my mind.

I want those kids to enjoy their underwear. Enjoy the selection. Enjoy being a kid. They are kids. I want them to be kids. To forget what brought them to our store.

I want what Jesus wants, for them to be cared for and loved.

We loved our day of service. We loved those kids. We loved the underwear. You can too.

Return for Deposit

I imitated Jesus the other day. Instinct. Not forced. No one told me to do it. It just happened.

It happened while my wife and I delivered our monthly meals to those in need.[41] Three hours devoted to service. To kindness. Our delivery families have become relationships. Friends. Our deliveries have become routine. Normal. Circled on our calendar.

Service needs to be routine.

One particular Tuesday, we passed a man rummaging through a dumpster. Three miles from our home. Close. Practically next door. We couldn't see him, only cans and bottles flying through the air. He was on his "normal" route, collecting aluminum cans and bottles for deposit and cash. His route included this dumpster, next door to our delivery family.

Before I knew it, my instincts took over. $20 bucks lighter. Passed off to a man, a family, in need.

Gracious, smiling, unassuming, this hardworking man received my Christmas gift. My present to him. I gave from the bottom of my heart. He graciously received.

When you give for all the right reasons, those who receive, receive for all the right reasons. They sense you truly care. It shows. It showed in his eyes, it showed in his expressions, it showed in his body language. When an act of love of others becomes routine, a habit, it shows.

Memory deposit.

I will not forget that encounter, that show of thanks. Perhaps the recipient will not forget our act of grace. My heartfelt routine. His Christmas was better.

Deposit.

Deposit for return. Return of joy from God in our heart.

This gentleman's routine, his day of collecting cans for food and shelter, was not routine that day. My day was changed as well.

My memory of his warm acceptance will remain. My vision of his family that evening. Smiling, thinking, praying. God knows and watches as that gift is used for his family. God witnesses our families' renewed spirit.

Imitate Jesus. Record memories. Share stories. God collected this deposit. A deposit I didn't know I was going to do. A routine reaction to a circumstance. A habit.

A habit that won't go away. Even in retirement.

Retirement. Renewed vision. What's to come?

Our past dreams centered around rest, relaxation, travel, multiple homes, leisure. Our vision now centers around service. Service to ourselves. Service to others.

Will we travel? Yes.

Will we relax? Yes.

Will we visit multiple homes? Yes.

Our travels will take us to needy homes. Our relaxation will center around comfort in caring for others. New and exciting people. Mission trips. Exploring God's Kingdom.

Like our encounter with this "can collector" of sorts, my wife and I strive to spend our time together, serving the Lord. Serving those around us. Serving those who may be *last in this world,* but will be first in the next. Building our Spiritual Portfolios.

Serve food.

Buy blankets.

Deliver meals.

Feed the hungry.

Build homes.

Mentor children.

Raise money.

Have a toy drive.

Have a food drive.

Embrace a cause.

Sort clothes.

Make a difference.

Visit prisons.

Adopt a child.

Volunteer.

Travel overseas.

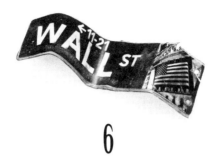

6

God's Checkbook: To Give or Not To Give

LESSON: Balance Your *Spiritual* Checkbook

God is My Bank Teller

Remember your first checkbook? Perhaps the first check you ever wrote? The first check actually made payable to you? Not the checks your grandparents sent you for your birthday—which were made payable to your mom or dad—but the first made payable to you?

I do. It meant everything.

I had opened my very own checking account. Straight out of college. My first job. My first paycheck. Made payable to me. A wondrous event. A memorable day.

Back in those days, "direct deposit" meant you drove straight to the bank with your deposit. The primary method of employer payment was via paycheck. I believe I was paid on a Thursday, with checks distributed at 2 p.m.

Magic. Money. Necessities. Food. Shelter. Clothing. Deposits.

All thoughts that raced through my mind. I could pay rent. I could eat. I could purchase another suit for my desk job. All items that mattered at the time, and still matter today. Getting paid was wonderful. The deposit more memorable. The physical action of getting this check into my bank account. An account barely meeting the minimum funds required.

Now, more than enough! More than I needed.

The deposit event was new. Noteworthy. Tedious. The bank counter. The teller. The endorsement. Careful signature by my nervous, shaky hand. The deposit slip from the back of my crisp new checkbook. Date of record, check #, deposit amount.

Standing in line. My turn. My teller. Guidance. Accuracy. Document review.

Deposit. Collected. Credited to my named, personal account at the local bank. My bank. My deposit evidence. My slip of paper. My record of deposit. First of many future deposits.

In those days, deposits mattered more than withdrawals. More than checks written for myself. Deposits meant a place to live, food to eat, clothes to wear, heat in the winter, air in the summer. Deposits were a basic necessity.

Let's return to that state of mind, that state of being, that state of heart, with our Spiritual Portfolio. Our checks should be for others, our deposits for our future. Our future with God.

God is our bank teller.

God is our deposit collector.

God carefully watches and records our deposits to the Kingdom. God cashes our checks for others. God accepts our "direct deposits" for deeds and service performed. God is pleased, even giddy about our initial deposits. He looks forward to many more He will collect on our behalf.

Big or small, God records.

New account or tenured depositor, God gathers deposits to your Spiritual Portfolio. Invested. Credited. Secured. Just like my initial paycheck, my initial deposit, my initial checkbook, God is pleased we discovered our account and embraced His Portfolio.

Deposits matter.

They matter for our earthly well being. Our eternal well being. Our spiritual focus on deposits matter to God and those around us. God carefully records our deposits, and is pleased.

Personalized Checks

Cashed checks. Checks from the past. Past expenses. In the good old days, we received our cashed checks with our monthly bank statement. A physical check showing the recipient deposited the check and received the funds. Subsequently, our check returned to our bank for payment. In turn, we received a collection of checks written over the past 30 days. A history of past actions. Past payments.

Many of those checks we write are personalized checks. Checks with some pattern, symbol, image, or identity that relates to us. Who we are. Our hobbies, our colleges, our pro teams. Checks can be personalized in any number of ways.

I prefer basic, simple, non-personalized checks from my checkbook.

Why?

God personalizes those checks written to my Spiritual Portfolio.

God collects and stores those checks for an eventual eternal bank statement. God will return those checks personalized. Those cashed checks, those mundane, simple, non-personalized checks, returned to me re-formatted.

Returned and personalized with images of lives changed, souls healed, children nurtured.

God's bank statement records our faithful activity and encloses our checks of changed lives. Checks with personalized images of deeds and donations. Images of families who benefited from our deposits. Images of the hungry being fed. Images of the cold with shelter. Images of the hurt, smiling. Images of God.

Consider bland, stale, lifeless checks. Checks that will be returned personalized from God. Personalized with your renewed energy for God's deposits. Personalized with your kindness. Your care. Your Kingdom. The Kingdom around you.

Sufficient Funds

Long before I had my first checking account, I wrote checks as a child.

Lots of checks. To lots of people. Checks I dreamed would be cashed. Not cashed for me, cashed for others.

My grandfather assisted in my passion. At an early age, I spent time with Papa. Quality time. Time with checks. Blank checks. Not fancy checks. Simple checks. Checks drawn on a bank that must have been out of business at the time.

Not in my young mind. I had checks. Real money. Real bank account.

I'd write checks to my cousins, aunts, uncles. Checks payable to my dad, my mother, my siblings. Carefree. Limitless. Endless bank balance. No bank reconciliation needed. It was fun, exciting, never ending.

I'm not sure where those checks ended up, if anyone deposited them, tried to cash them. Perhaps I should ask. My carefree attitude was the point. A generous attitude. An attitude that my check would be covered, would not bounce. An endless bank balance supporting my generosity.

Our Spiritual checkbook should have a similar outlook. Similar attitude. Similar generosity.

God will provide, God will assist, God will ensure sufficient funds. Our gifts of faith to others should have this child-like generosity. This interest in giving, this interest in others, this interest in writing checks to those who matter. God and others.

Show By Example

One morning I was busy in my home office shuffling papers, when my son walked in and asked, "What 'cha doing?"

I mumbled something about paying bills and writing checks, as he glanced down at a paper nearby.

"What's this?" he asked, as he picked up a piece of paper from my desk.

"Our record of contributions to the church," I said, in a casual manner, not thinking anything of it.

"Stop," I said.

"What?"

"Give me that." I motioned to my son, irritated.

He looked at me puzzled, yet in full recognition of what he had just read…our record of gifts we made to the church for the past year. His eyes wide open, he left.

Upon reflection, my initial reaction struck me in an odd way. My first instinct was to be very secretive about our gifts to the church. Later, I felt like, "Hey, wait a minute. We have given quite a bit, from our hearts, and having a record is a good thing." The church records it, and thankfully, so does God. We are blessed with gifts from God, and returning the favor is our goal. Even if I wanted to hide it, I couldn't.

God knows. God records. Our church records. Our charities record. We should be pleased to record our gifts to our Spiritual Portfolio. Our deposits. A deposit to my son's attitude of giving.

It turned out well. My son and I discussed what we had given to the church, how the money was spent (operations, missions, etc.) and who would benefit from our donations. I was pleased by what we were able to give to the church, by what God had given us and by what we returned to the Kingdom. Our conversation launched us into another conversation about giving in general. Unknowingly, my son's passion for giving started at home. Led by example. By action, commitment, responsibility. Deposit.

It's All About Change!

Whether checks or change, it all matters. It all adds up.

Donate your change. We do. We make a big production of it.

Our family has embraced change: physical change and literal change. We recognized that change, loose coins, had become wasted money. Change in buckets, dishes, cups, you name it. Pennies. Nickels. Dimes. Quarters. Even my children were against receiving change as their allowance. Dollar bills were the ticket. Paper money mattered.

In our house, change was everywhere. Multiple locations. Varying amounts. Uncounted but collected. Collecting dust. Too much change for the rare instance when we use parking meters. Better yet, who wants to shop with a pocket full of change?

Solution? Our charitable change sorter. Our family's purchase of what I defined as our charitable change collector. Yes, we bought a small, home version of the loose change sorter. What an impact! What a change it made. What a change it continues to make.

We embrace it. We deposit to it. We focus on it. What a difference it makes to our family, especially our kids.

Change all of a sudden became important. Loose change meant donations, deposits for those in need. A penny on the ground…absolutely picked up! We searched high and low for any

possible coins. My pockets. My briefcase. Mom's purse. Mom's currently unused purses. The sofa. The chairs. The change dish in the car. Everywhere.

Did we pay cash? Good...the change meant donations. Deposits to our charitable change sorter.

We are on a mission for change! We hawk for coins. We want change in the sorter. I think the kids like the accumulation, the process of seeing loose change become meaningful. Meaningful to others.

We select new charities each time the sorter is full. A new place to bring our collected community of coins.

Ever place a roll of quarters in the offering plate? Better yet, ever let your children drop a roll of coins in the basket?

Try it.

Watch the eyes of your children. Watch as they monitor that roll of change drift away in the plate, to those in need. Watch the smiles. The comfort. The sense of accomplishment.

Ever place multiple rolls of coins in the offering plate?

Try it.

It gets heavy.

Change has become a passion, a focal point, for our family. Change, and the collection of it, has become a simple way our family deposits to God's mission. Our collection of loose coins has brought about "change" in our lives. Change in our hearts. Change in our souls. We feel good when we deposit. We feel a sense of accomplishment when we deliver our rolls of coins to charities.

Those charities, those in need, they want it. They want the change. Big or small. One roll or multiple rolls. They want your collections of coins.

Those same charities want a change in you. Your change. Your changing heart, your changing identity, soul and character. Your changes on earth. All because of change.

Jesus-Like.

Speaking of change.

Others see the changes as well. The changes in you. Your new identity. Shaped by your commitment to God. Your commitment to deposits.

As you perfect your acts of faith, your acts of compassion,

your acts of justice, your character forms to what God intends. What God intended. What God wants in all of us.

Renewed character. A character tweak. A character makeover. We could all use a character lift. Our deposits earn God's earthly dividends in the form of renewed character. Revised lives. Rich, compassionate souls from the acts we perform for others.

Our deposits create our new identity. Our "Jesus-like" identity focused on others. An identity tied to gracious acts to those in need. A Jesus legacy. A Jesus attitude. A deposit attitude reflecting our Jesus-like identity towards others.

We may not be able to cure the sick, but our time and money could assist those in need.

We may not be able to make food for thousands out of a few crumbs, but our gifts can buy food for the starving.

We may not be able to travel around the world on mission trips, but our tithes can send those who can.

Study Jesus. See God's love for all. His love for others.

Our deposits reflect our Jesus attitude.

True giving is focused on the needy, not what the giver might receive in return. Giving based on anticipated selfish gain has missed God's investment opportunity, His purpose in charity.

Give to live a fuller life. Give to live a life that has meaning.

Giving to gain a quick return on deposit is destined to fail. Give because God asked that you give. As we embrace giving, this act of charity, God changes our lives. Heartfelt giving provides God's return on deposits. God's return on investment earned for eternity.

Financial gifts are also deposits to God's Spiritual Portfolio. Our checkbook recognizes that the needy, the poor, the destitute, require financial resources to survive.

Should we give money to the beggar on the street corner?

God says *yes*.

Give. Simply give. Don't wonder or worry if the beggar will make good use of the funds. Allow God to guide this needy man. Make your deposits. The return will be provided later in life. In eternal life. In renewed spirit. In the here and now.

Why don't we give?

Our pride. Our self-centeredness. Our greed diverts us from truly embracing God's mission. God's request for deposits to His Spiritual Portfolio. We must reverse our consumption. Return those treasures that God provided us on earth.

Donald Miller puts it this way, "My life testifies that the first thing I believe is that I am the most important person in the world. My life testifies to this because I care more about my food and shelter and happiness than anybody else's."[42]

We cannot take our treasures on earth with us to Heaven. But we can bring a little Heaven down to earth with us now. If we focus on our wealth at the expense of Heaven, we lose Heaven altogether. God provides us a chance to shift our portfolio strategy to earn His eternal rewards. And start enjoying them now.

Shifting the focus from ourselves to others.

Jesus did it. So should we. Jesus and His disciples focused on others first, themselves second.

God gives us choices. Daily choices. At work. At home. A choice to eat from any tree…but one. A choice to serve. Mission choices. God extends this choice moment by moment.

Our checkbook is a choice. A choice to hoard. A choice to give. A choice to ignore. A choice to embrace. "For where your treasure is, there your heart will be also."[43]

Our choices make our lives. Future choices. Past choices.

Good ones. Bad ones.

God offers us a choice to change. A choice to make a difference. A choice to spread the fruits of our labor to God's Kingdom. A deposit. The deposit. A deposit that will reap eternal life rewards. Endless dividends. Endless interest. Kingdom gains.

> **Our checkbook is a choice. A choice to hoard. A choice to give. A choice to ignore. A choice to embrace.**

Our choices aren't easy.

The more we think we need, the more we ignore those in need.

We're anchored. We're in control. We want more. Need more. We must release. Look in the other direction. Undo what is done. Greed is thirst. Thirst for more. Never quenched. Our hearts change from their original form. Our hearts harden.

Our hearts should be soft.

Selfish action hardens hearts.

Unselfish service softens. Generous gifts renew.

Include. Don't exclude.

Serve before you give. Develop passion about a cause.

Embrace your Spiritual Calendar in an effort to energize your Spiritual Checkbook. Passion for giving comes from service and mission. Develop passion by serving. Launch giving by seeing.

Do gifts matter? Do tithes matter? Do loose coins matter? God recognizes donations, big or small.[44]

- SoupMobile can feed a homeless person with $1 ($10 for 10 meals).[45]

- North Texas Food Bank sends children with a weekend backpack of food for $4, and can feed a family of four for a week on $20.[46]

- Agape Clinic can provide medical clinic expenses for a family for $25.[47]

- The Evangelical Methodist Church in Costa Rica can feed a child for a week in Los Guido for $10.[48]

- One month of school for a child in Matamoros, Mexico costs $35.

- $10 will provide blankets and warm clothes for a family this winter.

- Malaria nets for a family in Africa costs $10.[49]

The average American spends up to $1.80 a day for a cup

of coffee.

We can afford it.

God seeks compassion. Passion in our giving.

God also seeks change. Change with our deposits. Change that truly impacts those in need. God seeks justice. Deposits of justice that transform the landscape for the poor. Deposits that change societies that either produce the circumstances or oppress them further.[50] Deposit as a form of compassion: aid to the poor, food for the hungry, healing for the sick, clothes for the naked. God seeks our compassionate deposits. Our deposits of kindness.

Deposit to educate. Deposit to innovate. Deposit to provide solutions to the recurring needs you see around you. Focus on change and justice. Focus on providing assistance and providing solutions. Solutions to empower. Solutions to change.

The second half of our Spiritual Portfolio is sourced from our checkbook. Our Spiritual Checkbook. God's bank balance. Our financial deposits that center around giving. Our Gifts and Tithes for the Kingdom. We will examine why we should give, how much we should give and to whom we should give.

Along the way, you will discover you can continue to focus on your Earthly Portfolio while embracing your newly discovered Spiritual Portfolio.

Recognize and understand: *The more you spend, the more you think you need. The more you give, the less you realize you need...and want.*

Our journey of faith starts with this recognition. This knowledge of God's Will for us. The knowledge of being in His Will. Just as Jesus knew His path throughout the gospels, we know our path while here on earth. Until we understand our true path to Eternity, we will remain focused on our Earthly Portfolio.

We must re-examine our Earthly Portfolio in light of God's provided Spiritual Portfolio.

Stop comparing. You'll stop consuming. Stop looking across the street. See what you have. Be content with what you have. Be blessed with what God has provided.

How?

See others in need. Live humbly. Find the pain. Focus your attention across town. Across the tracks. Not on your neighborhood. To the back of the line.

To *balance your Spiritual Checkbook*, you must reverse your priorities. Reverse your expenses. *Reverse the order.*

7

Reverse the Order

LESSON: Pay ~~Yourself~~ *God* ^ First

Charity in the Christian faith means love,[51] to love one another, to provide for others at our own expense. To provide for others at our own expense, we must humble ourselves before the Lord. To efficiently humble ourselves before the Lord, we must act in obedience. Obedience to God is to live as Jesus lived. To focus on those in need, the poor, the destitute. Charity.

Obedient giving is not designed to earn our eternal reward. Obedient giving is designed to humble ourselves, thus living more as Jesus did during His time on earth. As we focus on Jesus' acts while on earth, we will find true obedience to the Lord.

Giving is an obedient act. Let go.

Our treasures on earth are temporary. Not ours. Treasures are given to those who will truly put them to God's use. As we give, we recognize that what we have, we do not need. As we recognize our temporary unneeded treasures, we truly embrace giving that earns Godly dividends for our Spiritual Portfolio.

> "There's no way to the presence of Jesus without the dying to self."[52]

To truly embrace giving, we must embrace others.

Our pride and conceit breed possessiveness, control, insecurity, longing. A clutching of sorts, to material possessions. Leaving many of us with large bank balances, debt, overstuffed earthly portfolios…and an empty earthly life.

> "So if you have not been trustworthy in handling worldly wealth, who will trust you with true riches?"[53]

In an act of obedience and true humility, we should shift resources to our Spiritual Portfolio, realizing and embracing the fact that we are loved by God. Who we are and what we have is just as God wants it. Our reflection is God's vision of us. To truly embrace ourselves as we are—to truly embrace what we have already—we must love others as Jesus loves us. By loving others, we see how to love, and we see His image in us.

> "...If I am not immersed in the reality of this Kingdom of love, it will not seem good or right to me to forgo reputation, pride, vanity and wealth, and I will inescapably be driven to pursue them."[54]

We search for and pursue earthly possessions based on insecurity about ourselves, what we have, and what we don't have. We see ourselves, our physical bodies, as having an end. We see our bodies, our lives, ending on earth. Until we recognize that our lives, our spirit, our hearts will live in eternal life with God, we will remain focused on ourselves. Our pleasures. Our collections.

Pursuit. We must realize that we are loved by God before we can give up pursuit. Otherwise, we will pursue all these feelings, these possessions, before our physical life ends. Thus we constantly seek, we long for acceptance in this world. Wealth in this world. We obtain. We collect. We remain empty. The more we long for different methods of material pleasure in this physical life, the more we realize what we search for is unreachable. Unattainable. Unquenchable.

Our constant pursuit of new passions lead us to never really gain at all. Instead, we collect items, possessions, portfolios and relationships. All to be left behind. As a result—in this physical, ending world for many of us—there is hopelessness.

The rich still search. The poor still search. Those who focus on earth, get earth. That thirst, that desire, endless. Consuming.

We must love ourselves as we are. We must love what we have. We must love God. We must recognize God's love. Until we do, we will focus here on earth. To focus elsewhere, is to love. To regain internal security about ourselves, is to love. Love others. Be loved.

Be loved by God. Be loved by Jesus. Be loved by our actions. Be loved by our deposits. Deposits for later use. Eternal use. Treasures not left behind. Saved for eternal life.

God's love, our love of others, re-instills security in ourselves. Our future. Our deposits focus on others. Our return on deposit focuses on us. A returned sense of security in ourselves.

Love is the key to finding security on earth. Love by God, a love of God and a love of others.

Our deposits are eternal. Our deposits are love. As we focus on depositing, we bring Heaven to earth. Heavenly focus produces earthly comfort. Earthly security. A security in our eternal lives, a security in our relationships, a security in what we have and who we are. In a word, love.

Agape love.

God's love. Unconditional. No matter what. Love that reaches others. No matter the circumstances. Always there. To love others is to *not only* love those around us (those in our circle of life, such as family, friends, workplace), but to love those who we don't know. To love those who don't love us. To love as God loves. No matter what. No matter what has been done. No matter whether or not you are loved in return. To love regardless, as Jesus did, is agape love.

To love as Jesus taught, we must *not* seek approval of others. We must perform good deeds for "an audience of one"…God.[55]

Actions to gain reputation, to gain approval from others, to glorify ourselves, are not deposits, but withdrawals. We must deposit for God. Simply God. Our deposits are not meant to seek reputation or some form of approval from others. Our deposits, heartfelt and deep down, are for Him. No one else. God is our tape recorder, our VCR, our DVR. Our Spiritual Portfolio is for His eyes only, but as we deposit, others witness it, imitate it and change.

"True" deposits are made from the heart, seeking no audience other than God. His Spiritual Portfolio is our goal. Glorifying His portfolio with our good deeds on earth. Our mission in the Kingdom. With a true "audience of one," along the way, others will see. Others will notice our heartfelt acts, and perform them as well.

God will record our acts of faith. Our deeds become second nature. Our love becomes agape. Our interest lies only in truly helping those in need. No self interest. No self promotion. Our deposits are for God and our Spiritual Portfolio. Our deposits are for others, not ourselves. Our deposits glorify God and His Kingdom, not ourselves in front of others. God records our deposits, performed in this way, to our Spiritual Portfolio.

Our true, heartfelt, selfless deposits are designed to glorify God, His Kingdom and those we are serving. Our deposits are registered by God, recorded by God, seen by God. Credited to our Spiritual Portfolio. Played back to us during our time with God in eternity.

Focus on true deposits. Avoid self-motivated withdrawals. Build a solid Spiritual Portfolio.

This earth has turned us into hard hearted, suspicious, self-centered individuals. Turn over a new leaf and live as Jesus did…caring, serving, donating, loving.

How do you do it?

Reverse the order. Reverse your checkbook. Reverse course.

Give. Save. Spend. Give again.

In that order.

Giving is a choice. To give is to love, to love is charity and charity is to give. God calls us to give. We have a choice to give, not an obligation to give. God judges our hearts, as we give, and as we build our Spiritual Portfolio.

Saving is a choice. To save is to defer. Deferring the enjoyment of your resources—be it earthly savings or eternal gifts— requires that we re-prioritize our checkbook.

> **Reverse the order. Give. Save. Spend. Give Again.**

Give first, save second, spend later.

Let's use our home as an example. To each his own, however, here is how we prioritize in our home:

Give First. Simply put, ensure that the first checks you write are for deposit to your Spiritual Portfolio. Paycheck deposited, gifts (checks) written (deposited to our Spiritual Portfolio). Be it charities or your church. Do not put these gifts off for later, such as your next paycheck. There is no IOU with God. He owes us nothing, and we cannot "owe" Him gifts when convenient. These deposits feed our spirit. Our gifts are a no-brainer…we do it. We deposit to our Spiritual Portfolio. Our goal is to ensure our initial 10% is out the door. To the doorstep of those in need.

1.   Paycheck enters our home (deposited);

2.   10% deposited to our church and/or our church's missions in the form of a tithe (poof… off to the Lord…deposit, it's that quick and sudden).

Save Second. Gifts to your Earthly Portfolio. Gifts for your "traditional retirement." Assets set aside to serve. Dollars set aside to live. To truly live. Reset your goals. "Save to Serve" rather than "Save to Spend."

3.   20% or more deposited to our family's Earthly Portfolio. Gone for another day…hopefully a day this Earthly Portfolio enables us to serve (i.e. rather than "Save to Spend" at some point…we "Save to Serve" and mission).

4.   Debt. To truly live, strive to live debt free. Should you have debt, consider deposits for debt reduction. Another choice.

Your choice. Live within your means. Your blessings.

Spend Third. On yourself. On your family. As your focus shifts from your Earthly Portfolio, to your Spiritual Portfolio, you realize how much less you need. How much less you want. How much more you want for others.

5. The Balance (the remaining dollars in your Spiritual Checkbook) is for our family spending budget. Our spending is guided by the deposits we make to our Spiritual Portfolio. Our giving and our service to the Lord. The more we see the need for our gifts and our service, the more we will recognize the less we need to live on. You will spend less here, and focus more on giving again…#6.

Give Again. Yes, once you recognize the beauty of your gifts, you will want to give again, i.e. generous giving. Will you give away too much for your own sake? I doubt it.

6. Give Again. Yes it happens. We want to give again. The more we give, the more we experience the joy of giving. The more we give, the less we need. The more we experience those in need, the more we want to help. Our service and mission work allows us to experience the need. The need to give generously.

To reverse the order, to change our spending habits, we must shift our focus to others. Release our anxiety, our doubt in what we have. Recognize our greatest obstacle is ourselves.

Confident in our path to eternal life, we will embrace deposits to our Spiritual Portfolio.

Commit to reverse your order of consumption. Commit to tithe. Commit to give generously. Commit to *paying God first.*

> "Remember this: Whoever sows sparingly will also reap sparingly, and whoever sows generously will also reap generously. Each man should give what he has decided in his heart to give, not reluctantly or under compulsion, for God loves a cheerful giver."[56]

8

Spiritual Deposit: Faithful Gifts

LESSON: Invest in ~~Your~~ ^Our Future

Christians are called to give. It's in our blood. Our desire to help others, to help other missions, to assist our church in spreading the Word of God.

Christians are called to reverse. To reverse our spending. To place God and others first. To tithe to the church.

Gifts to God's house. For God's mission. Gifts based on mercy, justice and freewill. Gifts in response to God's grace.[57] Gifts that share blessings with others and those in need. Gifts that seek Christ.

Seek Jesus. Seek Him in a place that He loves. His church.

Your church. Jesus loves church. The mission of the church. Tithe to have a place to worship Him. Tithe out of desire to seek Him. Tithe because Jesus asks you, not because He makes you. Tithe as a reflection of your giving nature, your motivation for God's eternal rewards.

Your tithes produce your church. Your tithes fund mission. Your tithes fund service. All through the church. Think of the church staff. The utility bill. The water bill. No light. No Sunday school. No worship. No learning. No Jesus. Love Him through your Tithe, your gifts to the church. The church is yours. For YOU. Seek and enjoy Him. Worship Him. Your location of community. A community of believers.

Here's the Church. Where's the Steeple?

What must it have been like? The beginning. The start. The inception. The origin of the Church. Can anyone really trace the first moments? The church that grew out of those first days following Christ's sacrifice. Those first few months following Jesus' death and resurrection. Historians have. We could.

Let's imagine it.

Let's envision it.

Let's create it in our minds.

A gathering. A group of people. One agenda. One reflection. One Jesus. What He taught. What He saw. What they saw. Direct witness to Jesus. Knew Him personally. Spoke with Him. Walked with Him. Learned from Him.

Followers, believers, addicts to Jesus' actions and attitudes.

Now, no Jesus.

A "Now what?" attitude. A "What do we do now?" attitude. A "Where do we go?" attitude. Believers who dropped what they were doing. Plucked from their profession, from their trade, from their livelihood. Left their homes. Their towns.

Especially the 12. A congregation of 12. The original 12. All focused on Jesus. Devoted to Jesus.

Now, no Jesus.

I can hear it now. I can see it now. Blank stares. Shifting seats. Looking for a leader.

"Let's meet." "Let's sit and discuss." "Let's figure out what it all means." A "No turning back now" feeling. A queasy feeling. Uncomfortable future. No direction. Questions. Doubts.

"I haven't fished in over three years. I sold my boat. The competition has moved in. New nets? New sails?"

Or,

"Tax collection? I haven't collected in years. I sold my booth. My collection bins. I'm not sure they would have me back."

You get the picture. You see where this is heading.

The early church was a discussion. A meeting to remember. A meeting to plan. A meeting of decision. A meeting to continue the mission. Jesus' mission. A meeting to delegate.

When to meet again. Where to meet again. Determine the message. Select the presenter. Set the agenda. Review the map. Solidify transportation. Food. Clothing. Water. Shelter.

On and on. Endless.

Some of them had trades, professions, jobs, roles in the community. Some didn't. Some just followed. Some just believed. Some were in need. In need of food and clothing. In need of the spirit of Jesus.

> "All the believers were one in heart and mind. No one claimed that any of his possessions was his own, but they shared everything they had…There were no needy persons among them."[58]

The early church remembered. The 12 reflected. They passed on His message. His mission. Those who were closest to Him. Those who spoke with Him. Those who knew the original teachings. Time needed to study, reflect, write, preach, travel, answer questions, teach. Collections needed for food, clothing, shelter, mission.

Spread the message.

Small gatherings. Small villages. Small fellowship.

The early church was a community of believers. A community of followers. Sharing their thoughts, sharing their memories, sharing Jesus. What He did. What He stood for. What He wanted us to do as His disciples.

Today's church is no different. Today's church continues. Today's church extends. Today's church passes on memories. Memories of the initial 12. Memories of those who followed. Those who wrote. Those who preached.

Our gifts and tithes continue that early church. Continue what Jesus taught. Continue Jesus' mission. Our gifts provide a community for believers. Our gifts teach, share, offer a glimpse into what the early church was like.

Enjoy the church. Enjoy your church. God does. God did. Remember the purpose. Remember the early days. Reflect on the struggles, and your gifts and tithes will mean more. More to you. More to those around you. More to your kids. More to your community. Tithe to enable the modern day message to be delivered.

Be the Church.

Big churches. Small churches. New ones. Old ones. Denominations. Teachings. One common thread. One message. One mission. One Jesus.

Jesus had no church.

No place of worship.

He was worship.

We started churches. We formed them. Congregations. Sunday school. Pulpits.

Why?

To gather together. To pool resources. To worship. To reflect. To remember. No agenda. Just Jesus.

Two thousand years later. Pooled resources. Giving to others. Giving to mission. A group of people committed to the memory of Jesus.

Tithe to retain. Give for the memory. The memory of Jesus. The tradition of the first church. The first group of people.

In a village. Sharing a meal. Remembering.

In remembrance.

Commit to the Kingdom

Define Tithe. Is there a definition? An exact answer?

No.

You define it. We define it. God asks that we determine. That we decide.

Is it the church? Is it mission? Is it teaching?

God wants commitment. God wants gifts for the Kingdom. Gifts for God and God's House.

A House that's everywhere. A Kingdom that's around us.

Consider direct gifts to God's House. Consider tithing as a percentage of our income to the Lord. God asks that we give according to what we have been given. Give out of joy that we are forgiven, not to earn our forgiveness. [59] Give out of gratitude for our blessings on earth. Our blessings of life. Of family. Of relationships. Of financial resources.

Does our Spiritual Portfolio require cash gifts?

No.

Should we give based on our ability to give? On our commitment to reverse?

Yes.

Must it be a certain percentage?

Generous Giving® states in their position statement on tithing, "God's standard for our generosity is not a percentage; it is obedience to the radical command to love others as we love ourselves, imitating the pattern of Jesus' radical sacrifice on our behalf...the New Testament does not give us a mandatory percentage for Christian giving. The apostle Paul says 'Each man should give what he has decided in his heart to give, not reluctantly or under compulsion.'"[60]

God's House is a fellowship hall of other followers. Other believers. Our tithes enable active members to mission and to share. To deposit those resources for the needy on our behalf. With our tithes, God's followers gather to spend those resources. Those blessings. Those heartfelt gifts.

Busy? No problem. Use the church. Giving to the church

is passive giving. Examine your soul. Explore and research the mission, the teaching, the impact of your tithes. Spread your heartfelt Spiritual Deposits to those focused on the missions of your church. Those acting on your behalf. On God's behalf.

How much and where to begin?

Start with gifts to the church. The missions of the church. Start with 10%. Yes, the Lord asks that we start somewhere. To reverse. To invest the first 10% to our Spiritual Portfolio in the form of a Tithe. A faithful gift. As we embrace tithing and giving to our church, we embrace our church's mission. God's ultimate purpose. Our focus shifts to our own budget and expenditures to enable us to pay these tithes. These generous gifts. We see God's wisdom in our true generous giving. We give first. We spend later. We make a commitment to Jesus. His life on earth. And we reap dividends on our deposits. Enhanced lives. Enhanced Jesus.

Heaven to Earth

> "…church doesn't exist for the benefit of its members. It exists to equip its members for the benefit of the world. To do that, it is about three things: community, spirituality and mission."[61]

Our churches provide an avenue for service and mission. Our calendars could be filled with hours spent helping others. Meal Delivery,[62] Soup Kitchens,[63] Affordable Housing,[64] Prison Ministry,[65] the list goes on. Our deposits are not to earn a reward, but to return a favor. Return the blessings we have received from our Lord.

Rob Bell, in his book, *Velvet Elvis*, presents a clear and distinct reason for generous giving and generous service. Basically, we see Hell on earth. We see poverty. Suffering. Homelessness. As faithful followers of Christ, we should desire Heaven's return to earth as soon as possible. We should live and organize our lives to bring Heaven to earth. Now. This attitude should reflect in our giving.[66]

Our Spiritual Portfolio is a record of our lives. Our attempt to bring Heaven to earth. Bell states, "As a Christian, I want to do what I can to resist hell coming to earth. Poverty, injustice, suffering—they are all hells on earth, and as Christians we oppose them with all our energies. Jesus told us to."[67] Our gifts to these charities, these churches, these injustices on earth, will bring us closer to Heaven on earth. Heaven now. Heaven here.

In his book, *Mere Christianity*, C.S. Lewis reaches a similar conclusion. "If you read history you will find that the Christians who did most for the present world were just those who thought most of the next."[68]

When God reviews your Spiritual Portfolio, where will you stand?

What is the condition of your heart?

Our hearts need mending. Our hearts require change. As we deposit, we change. Our hearts change. Our faithful actions and gifts enable our hearts to soften. To nurture. To adjust. Deposits change hearts. The needy, the suffering, the injustice, changes our hearts.

Our hearts need a re-birth. To be re-born.

Our memory needs a re-birth. A reformation.

The initial step to a change of heart, is to see. To experience those around us. Those in need. The heart will change. The memory will change. We must focus on our inner being to truly live as Jesus did.

And that is to serve in the form of Deeds, Mission and Tithes to the church. When we deposit, we turn our hearts back to God. We turn our hearts back to Jesus for a re-do.

God wants a re-do. A makeover.

He knows the impact. Soft hearts change their surroundings. Soft hearts fuel deposits. Recognized deposits. Collected deposits toward our heart makeover. Perhaps a slight makeover. An extreme makeover. God wants the heart changing. Non-stop.

Continuous.

Daily.

Weekly.

Moment by moment.

If our memory fades, our heart hardens. Constant attention is required. Constant nurturing. Continuous depositing. Like our earthly portfolio, to enjoy the dividends, we must make deposits. We must make investments. We must examine, review, change and focus on the horizon. On the goal.

Much the same, we must continue to deposit to our Spiritual Portfolio. To ensure a Spiritual heart. To ensure a Spiritual memory. To ensure a portfolio that will earn dividends today. Tomorrow. Eternally.

Our deposits are a response to God's love for us. God's request that we love Him and that we love those whom He loves. Along our journey to building and nurturing our Spiritual Portfolios, we bring Heaven to earth.

Today.

A richer, fuller life. Now.

A life which is selfless, emotionally sound, financially secure and Spiritually focused.

> **Faithful Gifts bring Heaven — which is in good condition — to earth.**

Deposits build our Spiritual Portfolio. Deposits transform the here and the now. Deposits ensure a better life. Faithful gifts bring Heaven—which is in good condition—to earth.

Eternity awaits, full of rewards. Full of interest. Full of dividends. We look forward to spending those invested deposits. That return of capital.

God pays dividends. Along the way. That we can spend today. Dividends in the form of a better earth. A better place to live. A fuller heart. Loving heart. Transformed life. We reap His dividends, which encourage continual deposits.

Here and now? A content life? A life without worry about our financial future? Our eternal future?

What does that feel like? How are we transformed?

Do we see life differently?

A resounding YES. All of the above. Take a look.

Transformed hearts. Transformed lives. Our family. Just look at our examples. Our family service. Our family giving. Our family perspective that God asks for. That God wants.

God knows there is much pain, suffering, oppression and injustice in this world. God knows we cannot correct all that by ourselves. God simply asks that we examine our own hearts, our own lives and live according to His mission. His vision.

To love God, and to love others.

Our family financial portfolio never looked better. Our focus, my focus, has lifted from "How much do we have" and "How much do we need" to "Look how much we have" and "Look how little we need." Our focus needed to change. Our focus yearned for change. As we focused on Spiritual deposits (rather than our possessions and our portfolio), we began to realize how much we truly had. How much we could truly give.

Along the way, God watched, God collected and God smiled.

We smiled. We cried. We gave. Those we support, smiled. Those in need, smiled. Those who received, smiled.

You can smile. Start your deposits today.

Live as Jesus did, today. Live out His wishes: to love God, and to love others. Deposits to God, for God. Deposits to others, for others. As we focus on Spiritual deposits, we receive what I call the dividends of today: compassion, love, security, peace, joy, a transformed life in Christ.

To deposit takes practice. As Marcus Borg states, "Practice being Christian."[69] Practice depositing. Practice caring. Practice and deposit go hand in hand.

Practice as a group. Deposit as a group. Do things together. Mission as a group. As a family. As a Bible study group. As a Sunday school class. As a workplace. As a tennis team. You name it. Groups are important. Accountability. Sharing. Building. Team orientation. The more we practice, the more we deposit, the more we develop passion about what God is passionate about...others.

Need a little compassion in your heart? Need a little passion to deposit?

Find a church that you like. Get involved. Not just on Sunday. Get up and go. Middle of the week. On a Saturday. Find a pastor that you like. Find a preacher that you like. Find a church that's yours. Tithe to it. Support it. Deposit to it.

Find that community, that group of adults, that group of believers who you want to be around. Find that church doing mission work. Outreach missions. Local. National or international.

Find a small church. A large church. Go worship. Go practice. Go see what they do. How they do it. Find a church, then deposit.

Find a church that teaches. That offers courses. Courses on the Bible. The Old Testament. The New. Courses on religion, Paul's letters, Jesus. Courses on parenting, divorce, finances, marriage. Find that church, and deposit. Tithe.

Give because you found a home. Give because you found a good Bible study group, a lecture series, a like-minded group of believers. Give because you found a community, a church. Share what you have to enable your church to share what you love about it, to others.

Tithes are broad. Tithes belong to God's people. God's servants. Tithes belong not only to a church you enjoy, but to those groups and communities who deposit to God's Kingdom. Tithe to Christian ministries, Christian organizations. Tithe to those groups, those followers, who perform compassion, perform service, to those in need. Tithe to groups who build homes, minister to foreign countries and spread the faith. Tithe to groups who further God's causes. Your causes. Tithe to those groups who give to God's passion. Your passion.

Where is the best place to find Christian groups benefiting your Spiritual Portfolio?

The church. That church you either found, or are exploring. To give to God's people, to Tithe, we must serve. Our Spiritual Calendar is an excellent place to start. Our mission and service work is an excellent way to discover tithing.

Once you serve, you see. *Invest in our future*. Go see it. It's there for the finding, and the tithing.

9

Spiritual Deposit: Generous Gifts

LESSON: Make a ~~Living~~ ^ *Life*

Treasures in Heaven

Our treasures in Heaven, our deposits, are secured for eternity. A portfolio without limits and with everlasting tenure.

Unlike material wealth, fleeting success and temporary treasures on earth, our deposits, our Spiritual Portfolio, is eternal. Our focus—in addition to our well being on earth—should be to build and enhance this limitless treasure. This portfolio that will be forever recorded by God.

True deposits from the heart, for others and for God, become our legacy. Our legacy on earth. Our legacy in Heaven. Our

Spiritual Portfolio. Our secure treasures in Heaven, without need of a guard, a security system, a bank vault. Treasures free from viruses, free from a desire to protect it, free from a need to insure it. A portfolio funded and built on our view of what really matters in His Kingdom: loving God and loving others.

As we embrace our Spiritual Portfolio, our desire to deposit builds. Passion bubbles from our heart. Renewed spirit. Compassionate outlook. Selfless deposits. For those in need. Those whom God loves.

As we focus on deposits, we form a Christ-like persona on earth. The more we imitate Christ, the more we realize our insecurities. Our old lives. Lives of constant searching for possessions, limited treasures on earth and fleeting wealth. Old lives driven by unobtainable security.

As our Spiritual Portfolio is enhanced, our "needs" reduce. The more we give, the more we realize we can live without. The more we spend on "ourselves," the more we think we need. If our heart remains

> **Generous Gifts recognize what we have. Generous Gifts recognize what God has provided.**

focused on our reputation and wealth, our true purpose is lost.

Generous giving recognizes what we have. Generous giving recognizes what God has provided. God wants our hearts focused on His Spiritual Portfolio. Heartfelt giving that goes above and beyond. Giving that provides Heaven and Earth!

"For where your treasure is, there your heart will be also."[70]

Pay Day Loans

Our earthly treasures are loans. Temporary loans. Temporary in our hands. Temporary possessions. Temporary assets. Temporary liability. We owe it to someone. Someone else.

Who else?

Others. Those around us. Those in need. The Kingdom. Our IOU. Our IOG…I Owe God. We owe Him. What He's given us.

Our relationships are on loan.

Our loved ones are on loan.

Our treasures are on loan.

God eventually collects. The ultimate collection agency. He asks for payments. Deposits. Return of treasures.

The temporary nature of our lives, and treasures, will

eventually return to Him. Wait until He collects, or pay in advance. Deposit in advance. Give back today. Give back our loans. Our temporary assets. Make them permanent.

Invest in your future.

In the church.

Those around you.

The ultimate return on our life expectancy. Seek it. Enjoy it. Return it.

Easy to Please, Hard to Satisfy

The more we see the need around us, the more we want to give. The more we see the pain of those suffering, the more we extend. Images engrained in our memory. Images of others. Others in need. In need of our generous giving, our above and beyond giving. More than tithing, more than charity. More from us. To lose our selfish outlook, we must discover the need, and act.

> "'How do I escape from the cravings of my gluttonous, overindulged self?'… There's no greater bondage than living only for what I don't yet have and for the evasive approval of people who, frankly, I don't really know or care about and who will always have just a little more than I."[71]

We embrace service. We embrace mission and deeds. We secure our budget to enable us to save for ourselves and to tithe to the Lord.

Give again?

"God is easy to please, but hard to satisfy."[72]

Give to your heart's content. The more we give, the more we want to give. The more we serve, the more we want to serve. The more we explore the mission work coming from our tithes, the more we become involved. The more we deposit to our Spiritual Portfolio, the more we deposit to His Kingdom.

> "Christ says 'Give me All. I don't want so much of your time and so much of your money and so much of your work: I want You."[73]

Our deposits are not a certain figure. Our giving is not a formula. Our hearts must be devoted to the Lord. It's this deep devotion to Jesus that satisfies. Deep devotion to the Kingdom. It's this deep devotion to our Spiritual Portfolio, that God yearns for.

Painful Giving

Generous giving hurts. A type of giving that pinches. Giving for those hurting and in pain. We hurt as our giving opens our view of the pain and suffering in the world. As Jesus hurts. As God hurts. Sacrifice today for tomorrow. Sacrifice comfort to care for others' pain.

Generous giving comes from a recognition that we need less and less in this life. Generous giving acknowledges how much we truly have. How much we have been blessed. How much we can truly give. A painful recognition that we have absorbed, rather than shared. We have spent, rather than invested in others. We have kept, rather than given away. We should not hoard our wealth.

We should share it.

We should use it for God's Kingdom.

We should give it away.

Serve before you give. See before you share. Strive to unlock that passion to get pinched. Develop passion for a cause. Our Spiritual Calendar creates passion. Service and mission seeks those in need. Develop passion by serving and seeing. Passionate service produces generous giving.

> "If our charities do not at all pinch or hamper us, I should say they are too small. There ought to be things

we should like to do and cannot because our charities expenditure excludes them."[74]

Deposit until it hurts. Hurts our pride. Hurts our consumption. Hurts our security of being in control. Service and mission hurts. The act of seeing what has been there all along. Give because it hurts. Give because Jesus hurts. God hurts. Pain in others' suffering. God suffers by our lack of giving. Others suffer by our lack of attention.

Return God's blessings. Invest those assets. Share the wealth.

The more we give, the more we deposit. The more we deposit, the more we enlarge our Spiritual Portfolio.

God truly seeks a Spiritual Portfolio full of His gifts, the returning of His blessings. God desires our investments for tomorrow. He provides eternal returns. Eternal dividends. Eternal life.

The more we deposit, the more we hurt. The more we hurt, the less pain and suffering in the world. The more we suffer due to our giving, the more we walk as Christ walked.

Where do we deposit? Where do we invest?

Give to charities that tug. Charities that pull at your heart. God has no rules here. He seeks humble care for others. God asks that we let go of our resources. Deposit them to His Kingdom.

How much more?

Your heart will tell you. God will show you. Service and mission will lead you.

How about another 10%? Reverse the order. Reverse focus. Give first (10%), save second (10 to 20%), give again (10%), spend the balance. God provides. God will provide. God has provided. God asks that you share.

As a nation, how much do we give?

Giving USA™ 2008—a publication of the Giving USA Foundation™, researched and written by the Center on Philanthropy at Indiana University—estimated in 2007 we gave $306.39 billion, setting a new record. Our giving represents roughly $1,000 for every man, woman and child in the nation.[75]

We have done well.

We can do better.

We can give more.

Commit your lives to Jesus. Live as He lived on earth. We change as He changed the lives of others.

Why change?

Because 36.5 million people (7.7 million families) in this country lived in poverty during the year 2006. Poverty—in this study by the U.S. Census Bureau and defined by the Office of Management and Budget—is defined as a family of four living on $20,614 per year (family of three—$16,079; family of two—$13,167, and so on).[76]

We can do more.

We can afford to do more.

Compare our poverty statistics with the following: There are now more than 9 million "Millionaire" households in this country (those with a net worth of $1 million dollars or more, excluding primary residences).[77] 7.7 million households at the poverty level, versus 9+ million households with $1 million or more dollars.

God recognizes these inequalities. He desires change.

As stated in Randy Alcorn's *The Treasure Principle*, we should "Raise our Standard of Giving, not our Standard of Living."[78]

Instead of worrying about making a living, we should be *making a life.*

According to the U.S. Department of Labor, those in retirement (ages 65 and over) have the highest level of giving across all ages studied. Those retirees gave approximately 6% of their expenditures to cash contributions, charities, churches and other organizations.[79]

The largest transfer of wealth in the history of the world will occur during our lifetime: Baby Boomers in this country stand to inherit over $20 trillion during the next 20 years. Unfortunately, this inheritance is occurring while Christian giving has dropped to less than 2% of per capita income.

> "If $10 trillion transfers by inheritance during the next 20 years, and if every believer passing away in the next 20 years would leave a 10% 'final tithe,' total gifting to Christian needs by Wills would be an estimated $1 trillion. This is compared to the $12 billion currently being given through Wills and Trusts."[80]

Could our decision to give generously help the world at large?

> "According to the United Nations, it would take $50 billion more a year to provide everyone on earth with healthcare, nutrition, clean water, education and a clean environment. Baby Boomers with incomes between $200,000 and $1 million a year could donate that amount by giving just 2% percent more of their investment assets."[81]

Start something.

Feel passion.

Extend a hand.

Help others.

Teach others.

Counsel others.

Become a model for others.

Lose yourself.

Become selfless.

Love others.

Give up gain.

Give up comfort.

Take on mission.

Take on service.

Take on deeds.

10

Portfolio Review

LESSON: Past Performance ~~Does Not Equal~~ *Equals* ^ Future Results

The Red Box

As a child, I loved visiting Papa and Mema, my grandparents, my father's parents.

Freedom, strange land, strange terrain, strange area.

Yet familiar.

Familiar house, familiar love. Aunts, uncles, cousins, family. Together. Kind of weird, different. However, very loving.

One specific summer, I spent time alone with Papa and Mema. Time with each of them. No siblings. No parents. Just me. What a glorious week. What an impression this small window of time had on my life as a financial advisor. Probably a pivotal point in an early decision to become involved in finance. In money. In business.

Papa was a small business owner.

Numerous businesses. Some worked. Some failed. Didn't matter in the end.

Needs were met. Food was served. Children raised. A hard life, but it worked.

In God's eyes, successful.

Papa owned a series of self serve gasoline pumps. I really mean *self serve*. No attendant. No people. Simply a gas pump or two. At a pullover. Roadside. Gravel area. Gas station of sorts.

To pump gas at one of these "pay for fuel" stations, one needed bills. Dollar bills. $1s, $5s, or $10s. Much like today's vending machines, Papa's gas pumps collected bills for fuel.

Drive up, insert bills, pump gas, depart. No credit. No receipt. No air. No food. Just gas. What a concept!

Collection days were most memorable. Days when Papa and I set out to collect those deposits for fuel.

A very distinct memory. Red metal boxes. Special key.

My first collection mission was the most fascinating. Drive up. Insert key. Hold a large plastic bin just below the door of the red box. Collect. As we opened the door, bills gushed into our waiting collection bin. Numerous bills. Gobs of bills. Overflowing. Bursting out of the seams. Out of the red box. Into our collection bin.

Papa's bin. Cold, hard cash. Station after station. $1 bills. $5 bills. Dollar bills in general. Large, metal, red boxes bursting with deposits from passing motorists. Each red box. Every red box. Bursting with money. With deposits. Deposits for fuel—collected and exposed—by Papa and I.

Papa seemed happiest that summer. It wasn't the money. It wasn't me. It was the security of knowing he was taking care of his family.

Our Spiritual Portfolios may take many shapes, but I consider mine a red box. We know God collects. We know God records. We know God pays attention to our good, faithful actions on earth. Our deposits are collected in our red box. Our red box, so full, that it stretches the seams. Our red box that God wants us to review with Him. That God wants us to open with Him.

God has the key. God wants it opened to expose our wonderful deposits. Our lifetime gifts to His Kingdom. Our legacy.

Imagine the deposits, as God opens your door. Imagine the memories that will spill out. Imagine the lives you impacted. The good deeds you performed. Those you assisted.

Your legacy.

A legacy spilling out for you to view and enjoy. With Him.

Along the way—as we deposit to our red box—we gather fuel for our earthly lives. Fuel that enables us to carry on. Fuel for our spirit. Fuel that only God can provide in the form of peace, joy, contentment. Gasoline in the form of a restored soul, renewed heart, loving spirit. Fuel needed to continue to live as Jesus taught us: to love God and to love others.

God has our deposit chamber, our collection of dollar bills, and He returns fuel to our hearts for a changed life on earth.

Those Were the Days

My daughter and I enjoy looking over old photographs. When she was younger. When I was younger. Our memories are strong for those joyous times…the first bike ride, the first words "daddy," the first day of school. Infant photos. Toddler photos.

She believes she remembers those days. Our days. As her father, I remember them well. A simple glimpse of old photos allow us to fully enjoy moments from the past.

Guess what?

Upon reflection, I seem only to recall the good times. The good memories. Those blessed times. Joyous fatherhood. No stomping. No fussing. No back talk. Rather, simple memories of joyful times, and the photos to prove it.

Much like God must remember. His memory of our good times. Our faithful actions. Our loving nature. Caring for others. Forgetting our bad times, our mistakes, our sins. God only recognizes our saved soul and recalls our renewed life in Jesus Christ.

> "The Bible indicates that all believers will stand before the judgment seat of Christ to give an account of their lives...after we die, we will give an account of our lives on Earth, down to specific actions and words."[82]

God has perfect memory. God has perfect eyesight. He has witnessed our deposits, our hearts, our intentions. He wants to play back His memory of what He's seen in us. What He's witnessed since we gave. God recorded not only our deposits, but the aftermath. The impact. God will show us how our Spiritual

Portfolio truly touched the lives of others. He'll show us all the good that came and will continue to come from our deposits. Our good deeds and actions on earth.

God's photo album of those you cared for. The lives you changed.

Those you touched. Those gifts. Those hours you invested.

He wants you to see the dividends, the earnings, the lives you impacted.

Imagine. We made it. We're in Heaven.

What to expect? What about our Spiritual Portfolio?

What about those checks we wrote to the church, to those charities? The days spent in service, those countless hours spent in mission work?

Did it matter? Will it matter?

Do we believe we will be held accountable to the Lord?

As a nation, we seem to think so. According to the AARP study, almost nine out of ten respondents (88%) who believe in Heaven, think they will achieve it. Women are more likely to believe they will get into Heaven (91%) than men (85%). Additionally, those who consider themselves "very" religious, almost unanimously think they will get into Heaven (97%), compared to "somewhat" religious (85%), or "not at all" religious (75%).[83]

Our Spiritual Portfolio is witness to others of our faith in Jesus. Our gifts, our tithes, our deeds and our service. A testament to our earthly decision to follow Christ, to imitate Christ, while on earth. An interest in bringing Heaven to earth, and acting on that interest today.

No Steps. No Formulas. Just Jesus.

Our Spiritual Portfolio is not designed to place us on God's nice list.[84] Our Spiritual Portfolio is designed to reflect our faith, and whether or not we lived it. A statement to the world that we lived a new life, a different life, a life for Jesus.

> **Our Spiritual Portfolio is witness to others of our faith in Jesus.**

No formula for salvation. No guarantees. No list to check off.

> "Jesus was always, and I mean always, talking about love, about people, about relationship, and He never once broke anything into steps or formulas."[85]

Our Spiritual Portfolio is not, and will never be, a step by step formula for entry into eternal life. And it's more than a portfolio of good works. Rather, a collection of our obedience. An expression of our faith in His way of life. His Holy Spirit. A reflection of Jesus.

Prepare your Spiritual Portfolio. Make your deposits. Recognize your Portfolio Review could come at any point. At any time. Our consultation with our Lord. Be it our earthly death, or upon Christ's return to the earth. We must prepare and live as if today is the day. Our day.

> "Good actions are all that matter. The best good action is charity....good actions done for that motive, done with the idea that Heaven can be bought, would not be good actions at all, but only commercial speculations."[86]

Our Spiritual Portfolio builds a rapport with God. Our deposits are remembered. Our Father's memory of our good acts of faith, not our sins or inaction. His recollection of our good works on earth, reflected in His collection of our deposits. Our true intentions with those blessings God provided. Prepare for your review, His review of our works on earth.

Our Spiritual Portfolio.

Home Movies, Treasure in Heaven

We will rejoice with God in our works, collected and deposited by Him, to our Spiritual Portfolio. A collective review of deeds performed, gifts made. Like father and child, reminiscing over old photographs, our Portfolio Review with God will be the same.

A joyous recollection of our deposits. Our gifts. Our service. Our earthly mission to serve the Lord. God will remind us. God will show us. God will review the impact those gifts and deeds had on the recipient. On the Kingdom. On those in need. God asks that we share our blessings. Care for one another. Love our neighbors.

Imagine it. Look forward to it. Seek it. Anticipate your Portfolio Review. Your review with God. Imagine God showing us photos, images and movie clips of those people impacted by our gifts. Gifts to the homeless shelter. God shows us a clip of a homeless man, bitterly cold, being wrapped in a warm blanket. Warm heart. Warm feeling.

"So that's where the money went?"

And God will answer, "Yes my child."

Our gifts for inner city kids. Never knew the child. Never knew the money was spent on outreach camp.[87] God shows an image of a wonderful young lady in cap and gown, graduating from college. Giving the commencement speech. "I'm not sure where the funds came from, but that summer I spent in the outreach camp changed my life…turned my life around. I realized people loved me…and that I could be anything I wanted to be. If you are out there, thank you for the gift."

Our gifts and service for prison ministry.[88] God provides a picture of the inmate— recently turned back over to society— returning home from an interview. Recently purchased business suit and tie. New uniform. Approaching his home, opening the front door, searching for his wife inside. Kids gather. Eyes meet. He smiles. He got the job. Thrills. Screams of joy ring through the home.

"Good job, my child."

Good deed performed for the beggar at a stop light. Impulse reaction. Thought nothing of it. Never thought of him again. God did. God shows you this man's gift being spent at the grocery store. Buying what small portion of food his collections would afford. God shows his departure from the store. His "shelter of a home." His prayer before his meal. Guess who he's thanking? He's thanking God for you and your Good Deed.

Time spent in abused and abandoned children's ministry[89]. Kids you witnessed bruised, broken, in tears. Your gifts provided hope. God shows these children in various stages of happiness later in life. A new child with a new family, around the dinner table praying to the Lord; children enjoying school, chatting and talking on the playground. Someone loves them. You love them. God loves them. No more abuse. No more concerns. Now an adult, this rescued child, started a charity determined to raise additional funds to support abused children.

The Sunday School student you taught for years. Quiet. Reserved. You always wondered if the work performed, touched her at all. If it was worth the effort. God shows—on multiple occasions—this young child telling her father (over Sunday lunch) how much she learned from you; how much she got from the lesson; how she tells others in her school to attend her church. To hear you teach.

God asks that we embrace our Spiritual Portfolio today.

God asks that we commit to His Kingdom. Selfless giving. Selfless volunteering.

God will take care of the rest. God touches the lives who need it most.

Visualize what our blessings will do.

Don't dwell on what we gave up. Our time. Our wealth.

Dwell on what we gained. Our Kingdom. Eternal life.

To serve is to see. To see the world around us. To see other lives around us. To see other situations. Want to give more? Want to have more compassion? Want to live humbly? Go see stuff. Go see people. Go on mission trips. Go to a soup kitchen. Deliver meals.

Once you see it, you cannot *unSee* it. You cannot erase that memory. Permanently recorded. You will be reminded as you serve again—and as you consider giving—what you saw during that service or mission experience.

God sees it as well. He records. He retains. Our faithful actions. Our insights. Our intentions. Our heart. Our deeds. Our memories. Recorded.

When we see, we serve, we deposit to God's Kingdom. Let's continue to open our eyes to see.

Remember? Remember when you served? When you gave?

Their pain? Our pain for them? Their joy? Their contentment? Can you remember? Will you remember?

We need to remember. We need to see those in need. To retrofit all our humble actions into our memory.

God will. God looks forward to a time when He can play back His images of our faithful action to the Kingdom. Our Portfolio Review. A glimpse of our actions. The impact it had. We remember. We remember that feeling. That joy in our hearts.

> "This is why gratitude is so central to the life God made us for. Until we can center ourselves on what we do have, on what God has given us, on the life we do get to live, we'll constantly be looking for another life. That is why the word remember occurs again and again in the Bible. God commands His people to remember who they are, where they've been, what they've seen, what's been done for them. If we stop remembering, we may forget."[90]

God returns the permanent. Returns the temporary of old. He stored up your deposits. He awaits a review with you, His Portfolio Review. He saw them. He sees them. He recorded them. Your rewards await in Heaven. Waiting on you.

The loan was paid.

The Kingdom was served.

His memory filled with your faithful actions. Actions on

earth. Erased memory of sin. Permanent memory of deposits.

Look at them. Take a peek. Peek into what you have done. Those you have impacted.

His memory is permanent. Their memory permanent. You're in it. You're remembered.

You cared.

You acted.

You deposited.

God provides a review of our good works on earth. God shows how our deposits impacted those around us. Our performance record. The dividends earned on those we helped. All the good that came and will continue to come from our good deeds and actions on earth. Our deposits produce changed lives.

Glimpse of Tomorrow

What will it feel like? Our Portfolio Review. How will we react?

I've got an idea. We've got a glimpse. Our family received handwritten letters from outreach campers we sponsored to attend summer camp[91]. Kids who otherwise could not afford the cost. Kids who would otherwise miss the chance to leave the inner city and experience another life. A life where people cared. A life they could visualize as their own.

Although unexpected, the letters felt as if God wrote them. As if God guided their hand. God was writing letters to me, through His campers.

Words of thanks.

Images of kids smiling.

Kids realizing they could do whatever they wanted to in life.

I look forward to God's playback video. God pointing those campers out to me. God showing me their changed lives. Their happy, fulfilled careers. Their families. All a product of blessings granted by those who cared.

Camp counselors. Camp directors. We all made their lives better. We all made deposits to our Spiritual Portfolios.

Some of those changed by our deposits, will be in Heaven, where God will introduce us. We'll visit with those impacted by our deposits.

Some of those we've changed, will still be on earth, and God will allow us to see their new, changed lives.

Look forward to your review with God. Strive for that review with God. Deposit for that review with God! Where your Spiritual Portfolio is concerned, *past performance equals future results!*

11

Restore Life

LESSON: You Are Your ~~Financial~~ *Spiritual* ^ Portfolio

Eternal Timepiece

We are collectors. Passionate collectors. Collectors of things, items, possessions that will remain here. On earth.

Our passion goes to the "nth" degree.

During the holidays, I received a catalog of potential collections. Potential possessions. We all get them. We all glance through them. Be it grocery store flyers, department store catalogs, you name it. Each identifying with our basic desires: to collect, to possess, to own. Catalogs of items that we "want," but don't need. Material possessions. A desire reflecting an earthly

159

focus. An earthly passion.

This particular catalog showcased timepieces. Watches. Men's and women's. No ordinary catalog. Hundreds of pages of timepieces with price tags beginning at $5,000 and up. Watches that cost, routinely, $10,000, $20,000, $70,000 and $250,000 per timepiece.

Even those marked "price upon request."

Price upon request? Who would buy these? Why would someone buy these? Why would time be such an interest as to command these prices? Why did I get this catalog?

I can answer the last question right away...I am a watch lover. Always have been, always will be. My passion came from my childhood. My mother gave me a pocket watch. A special item. My first real timepiece. A magnificent, gold timepiece that I still own today. It sits on a shelf in my office as I type this passage.

Answers to the remaining questions, center on earth. Our earthly focus. Our focus on today. Tomorrow. This morning. Time at any given moment. Yes, we need to know what time it is. For appointments, for our schedules, for our lives. But to constantly monitor time in such a manner?

Our focus on time signifies our preoccupation with time remaining. Time left. Our time before death. Our time left to do those things we desire to do.

Our focus should be on time to live, time to serve, time to give. We should embrace time remaining. Embrace each day. Look forward to the time we meet Jesus.

At these prices, I would expect a watch that could tell us our time remaining. Our time left on earth. How much more time before we meet God? How much more time before we review our Spiritual Portfolios?

Perhaps, we as Christians would be better equipped to live God's mission—to love God and to love others—if we had such a timepiece.

What would that watch cost?

Would we be willing to pay for it?

As a watch collector myself, I envision this timepiece as a blessing, not a curse. A clock signaling when we get to meet God. A countdown until our Portfolio Review, our welcome meeting to study and reflect on our good works on earth.

A watch reflecting our desire to show God our good actions

on earth, rather than a watch indicating how much time we have left before death. A timepiece highlighting our time left to receive our rewards in Heaven.

A watch that God collects upon our arrival to His throne.

A watch that God indicates we no longer need. Eternity has no end. Time is not an issue. Never was. Once we accept Jesus, time becomes endless.

The next time you glance at your watch, think of eternity. Your eternal timepiece. God's timepiece of your time on earth. He knows when you will arrive. He has the appointment on His calendar. He won't miss the meeting. Neither will you. Plan for it. Look forward to it.

Fill your time on earth with Spiritual deposits. Watch time pass by unnoticed. Watch time fly by. When you Serve, Mission, Give, time escapes. Immerse yourself in deposits, and time becomes nonexistent. Nonexistent time. Just like eternal time. Never-ending time.

What time does your watch show?

Mine shows eternity. An eternity of time left with Jesus. With God.

The Final Exam

We know our time is coming. Our time with our Father. Our time to shine. Our review of His sight. His vision of our actions. Our appointment.

Advanced notice. Pop quiz without the pop. A test. An exam where we know the questions in advance. We know what is to be asked. What needs to be shown in our work. Our faithful actions. We simply have to perform. We have performed. We can perform more.

Bob Buford, author of the book *Halftime,* believes we will all face the final exam. Our examination with God. Our review of our Spiritual Portfolio. Buford states we know the questions:[92]

1.   What did you do about Jesus?

2.   What did you do with what I gave you to work with?

We know the questions. We know how to answer. We know how to deposit. We simply must begin.

Begin today. Prepare today. Study today.

As a Financial Advisor, I suggest quarterly meetings. Time spent with each client to review their situation, their goals, their wealth. We discuss how the portfolio performed, what deposits were made and what changes might be warranted. We determine whether or not we met the goals we set for ourselves.

We discuss whether something has changed in their life. Will there be less income, less deposits? Will there be more expenses? What areas do we need to focus on? What deposits were missed? What areas were overdone?

We should be no less thorough while evaluating the current state of our Spiritual Portfolio.

Our state of heart.

Our state of memory.

Where are we with our deposits?

Did we deposit too much money and not enough time?

Are we in a giving rut?

A service rut?

In my line of work, I often suggest that my clients review their portfolio allocation. Have they met their objectives? Have their objectives changed? Do we need to reduce our exposure to one type of deposit, and increase our exposure to others?

God, as our Heavenly Advisor, asks us the same. He asks that we continually examine the status of our Spiritual allocations.

Where does our giving stand?

Where does our tithing stand?

Where does our service stand?

When was our last mission trip?

When was our last good deed?

Have we lost our compassion? Have we tired? Grown weary? Lost interest?

Have we allowed our minds and memory to revert back to the old?

Do we see the world as gracious? As a gift from God?

If not, we should revisit our deposits. Refocus our efforts. Reallocate our priorities.

A Vision Beyond Ourselves

If we see life as gracious and unending, we tend to deposit. We tend to focus on the needs of others. "…A willingness to spend and be spent for the sake of a vision that goes beyond ourselves."[93]

If we see life as fleeting and ending, we tend to collect. We tend to gather, abuse and exploit. Our existence begins and ends here on earth. Our focus remains on ourselves.

Our view of life is exemplified in an annual review of our Spiritual deposits. Our Spiritual Portfolio should look beyond ourselves to the needs of others. A willingness to trust that all that exists does not end with earthly death.

Our deposits focus on relationships.

Relationships with others, relationships with strangers. Those around us. Those in need. Our deposits reflect our relationships with our money. Whether we view it as a possession or a loan from God. A treasure to be shared, or wealth to be hoarded. How we invest our deposits reflect our relationship with our church. How we invest our time, our tithes.

How we view these relationships ultimately determines how we view our Spiritual Portfolio, and what condition it is in at any given moment.

Our deposits to God show our love for God, and for those who God loves.

Those around us.

Those in need.

His church.

Your church.

Our deposits reflect our interest and care for those who God cares for. He wants to see our compassion and love for those He loves. He wants to collect. He wants to reward. He wants our constant evaluation of our portfolio of deposits to His Kingdom.

Why?

"We love because he first loved us."[94]

"..since God so loved us, we also ought to love one another."[95]

"God is love. Whoever lives in love lives in God, and God in him."[96]

Recognize this love by loving others. By depositing to our Spiritual Portfolio, we show our love for those He loves. God loves us, no matter what. No matter what we did. No matter what we have done.

Deposits are love. Unconditional love for others. Selfless deposits for others. God's Kingdom.

Evaluating Our Spiritual Portfolio

Our initial Spiritual Portfolio begins with a firm foundation. A foundation built for day to day needs. An initial set of deposits to establish our core beliefs for future growth.

Our firm foundation begins with a new attitude. A Jesus attitude. An "other" focused attitude. An attitude of kindness and caring toward others. A new heart. A new inner core that sees the needs of others, and acts.

Our firm foundation starts with our **Deeds**, our outlook on others.

We add **Mission** and **Service,** to broaden our perspective.

Through **Tithing**, we embrace Jesus and His message.

By **Generous Giving**, we seek lofty returns by going above and beyond.

Service. Mission. Tithes. Gifts.

Ensure proper deposits for all. They feed on one another.

Good deeds produce good feelings. Good feelings produce faithful service. Faithful service produces quality mission. Quality mission deserves quality resources. Resources require gifts. Gifts require compassion. Compassion thrives on service.

Service requires community. Community requires believers. Believers require worship. Worship requires tithes. Gracious circle. Continuous cycle.

God wants your attention to all deposits. Some more than others. Time, perhaps more than money. Money, perhaps more than time. It depends.

Some serve, some give. Some tithe, some mission. Depending on our life, our stage of life, our focus could change.

Find your niche. Find your focus.

But deposit to all.

Leave none out.

Leave your legacy. Jesus' legacy.

Use His example. His ministry. His disciples. He asked that we follow Him. That we copy Him. That we imitate Him. Do what He did, have faith and follow. He once told his disciples, "I tell you the truth, anyone who has faith in me will do what I have been doing."[97]

Our life is but a collection of choices.

Choices to lead.

Choices to follow.

Choices to deposit.

Choices to collect.

Choices to tear down.

Choices to restore.

If today were the day, what legacy would be left? What deposits were made? Whose memory did we affect?

Our choices are recorded daily. Recorded by God. He watches. He's prepared.

If God calls you home, can you truly say that you followed His example?

Did you serve and not give? Give and not serve?

How well diversified is your Spiritual Portfolio?

Our legacy starts today.

Look forward to your review with God. Look forward to seeing the impact of your deposits on the Kingdom. Seek to reap the benefit God provides in a changed heart. A sign of your future rewards in Heaven.

When reviewing my clients' portfolios, I discuss the benefits of multiple investments, multiple strategies. How they are different, diversified, yet compliment one another as a collection of cohesive assets with one common goal.

So too, are our Spiritual deposits. Different in type, yet connected and related in goal to love God and to love others. Deeds produce desire. Desire produces service. Service produces mission. Mission needs gifts. Gifts become tithes. Tithes make mission. Deposits reach beyond. Beyond ourselves.

Time to evaluate your Spiritual Portfolio?

Have a review. Host a review. Conduct a goal-setting session. Include your spouse. Include your children. Commit to be nice. Commit to perform service work. Alone, or as a group. Decide to donate. Decide to tithe. Determine a percentage. Determine a day of the week. Write it down. Review it. Embrace it.

Establish a goal, perform the goal and commit to the goal for 30 days. A month makes a habit. A habit to deposit. A habit for you. A habit for your family.

Revisit the goals. Reward yourself. God has. God will. God looks forward to His review with you.

What has God seen in your Spiritual Portfolio?

God sees your interests. Your heart. Your talents. Your deeds. Your faith in the form of works. God views your Portfolio

Allocation on a daily, weekly, monthly basis. Nonstop.

God recognizes that our Portfolio Allocations will change throughout our life. Interest levels change. Finances change. Time commitments change.

God simply wants commitment. Continuous. Throughout.

What should your Spiritual Portfolio look like?

Today? Tomorrow? Judgment Day?

How often should you reflect on your portfolio?

Should your deposits vary? Change over time?

Does God have a certain recipe? A specific solution?

God wants deposit diversification. God wants us to see the world around us. To see, serve and give. He wants participation in each deposit. Not just money. Not just time. He wants eyesight.

With our eyes on those in need, we want to serve. To donate. To help. Once we commit to see, we deposit. Our lives change. Our Spiritual Portfolios evolve.

Giving more than serving?

Rebalance. Redo your mix. Focus on service. Go see stuff. Go mission. As you commit more time to serve, your giving means more. You'll want to give more. You'll invest more.

What is God looking for?

Is there a recipe? A perfect set of ingredients?

No. God wants our attention. God wants our eyes. He wants our witness of what He sees in this world. He wants Heaven brought to earth. He wants deposits to His Kingdom. However small or large the gift, deposit it. Whether an hour or a week of service, deposit. He's not looking for a certain Spiritual Portfolio balance. Rather a commitment to deposit.

Big or small. Minutes, hours, or days. $5, $50, or $5,000. God wants our time and gifts.

To truly commit our eyes to deposit, we must give. Give our time. Give our money. Give of ourselves. Focus on others. "He must become greater; I must become less."[98] Selfless acts to those around us. As Jesus did, we should as well.

Deposit because you care. Commit to the Kingdom because Jesus did. Our Spiritual Portfolio is not a formula for eternal life. Our faith is. Faith is weak without deeds and service.

Deposit just because. Because you can. Because you want to. Because you're forgiven. Because you want Heaven on earth now…not later.

> "Not doing these things in order to be saved, but because He has begun to save you already. Not hoping to get to Heaven as a reward for your actions, but inevitably wanting to act in a certain way because a first faint gleam of Heaven is already inside you."[99]

Deposits. Earnings. Dividends.

Will you reap a reward?

Is there one?

Is there a goal in mind?

Yes…Heaven on earth.

Waiting for judgment is not necessary. Deposits allow us to reap rewards in our hearts today. Immediate rewards earned by our good works on earth. Our heart, our soul, our imitation of Christ.

> "The doctrine of eternal rewards hinges on specific acts of faithfulness done on Earth that survive the believer's judgment and are brought into Heaven with us."[100]

Certainty in life.

Certainty in eternal life for sure. God promises it. Deposits earning rewards. Focus on your Spiritual Portfolio, and your Earthly Portfolio will be cared for on its own. Spiritual certainty via deposits to your Spiritual Portfolio.

Dwell on what you've earned, not given up. Dwell on time invested to God's Kingdom. Dollars given to those in need. The Heaven you brought to earth. Dwell on your eternal life span. Uncertainty of life on earth, replaced with certainty of eternal life.

Heaven's record of your works.

God's photographs. His images. Those around you. Those affected by you. Your actions. Your gifts.

What does it look like?

Perhaps a book of portfolios. Book of deeds. Deposits. Depending on your heart, your intentions, your thoughts, your stage of life, your finances.

Open the Eyes of My Heart, Lord

There is a song we sing in our church from time to time which means a lot to my family. The lyrics are quite powerful: "Open the eyes of my heart, Lord...I want to see you."[101]

These lyrics speak to the longing I felt.

The emptiness.

The void in my heart.

That period when my balance sheet dictated my actions.

Everything I had worked so hard for, wasn't enough. *I've got it all...now what?* The search began. I groped for God. I shifted my focus to those in need. To those I could serve. I embraced my greed, but a different greed. A satisfying greed. Greed that was no longer about me. Greed that was greater than myself. I exchanged my greed for this world, for greed for the next. I wanted to see Him.

Greed can be good.

Greed for God is good.

How do we see God?

How do we open our hearts to see what God does for us and those around us?

We open our hearts to see God through our actions for others. Our deposits to His Kingdom. If our hearts are hard, we shut down, we focus on ourselves. We focus on things. We collect. We hoard. We focus on our net worth instead of our *self worth*. If we open our hearts through deposits, we see God, and He sees Himself in us. We become our true selves. What He intends. In His image. His example. And we *discover our Spiritual Portfolio.*

Not only do we need to see God, our world needs to see God. Our world needs to see God through us. Our world needs to see our deposits. Our deposits of time. Focused on others. Invested on others. We fill our calendars with time spent at work, at home with our family, with friends.

But are we focused on *God's Calendar*? Are we focused on continuing to emulate Him in service? To love God is to love whom He loves. Depositing to His Kingdom. Deposits that benefit the world. After all, *time for God is money.*

He longs to see more deposits. Deposits in response to His calling to have compassion—to rediscover love, to love one another—and to embrace those around us. To find happiness in doing good for others. Selfish about service. About mission.

Good Deeds are unselfish acts toward others. *Good Deeds* are a direct result of your compassion for those around you. Kind words, kind smiles and kind thoughts will develop that compassion.

Unconditional service. Unconditional deeds. Merciful deeds to others.

So you don't feel like it? Do it anyway. Jesus was tempted to ignore those in need. He was tempted to turn the other direction.

But He didn't. He continued to serve. That's His message. Compassion, service, others. Remind yourself, "It's not about ME, *it's about YOU.*"

Change your purpose. Change your perception.

Lose your agenda.

Lose yourself.

Restore your life.

Go on a mission trip. *Big Deeds*. Planned in advance. Time dedicated to spread hope to the world. Imitate Jesus. Make your mission, your service, routine. Serve those who may be *last in this world* but will be first in the next.

The decision is ours.

A decision to ignore. A decision to embrace. A decision to be first in this world.

Or a decision to be last.

God asks that we deposit to His Spiritual Portfolio. He wants our faithful service. He watches, records, retains our actions. Our intentions. Our *Big Deeds*.

Our first job. Our first paycheck. Our first deposit. Those were the days when deposits mattered more than withdrawals.

Deposits for a place to live, food to eat, clothes to wear, heat in the winter, air in the summer. Deposits for basic necessities. God wants us to return to that state of mind with our Spiritual Portfolio. Our checks should be for others, our deposits for our future, our future with God. *Balancing our Spiritual Checkbook* shifts focus from what we have, to what we can give.

And that means stop comparing.

If we stop comparing ourselves with others—stop looking across the street—we'll stop consuming. We'll be content with what we have. We'll recognize the blessings God has provided.

We pursue earthly possessions based on insecurities. About ourselves. What we have. What we don't have. We see ourselves— our physical bodies—as having an end. Until we recognize that our Spirit—our hearts—will live in eternal life with God, we focus on ourselves. Our pleasures. Our collections.

We must realize that we are loved by God before we can give up the pursuit.

How do we turn over a new leaf? How do we live as Jesus did?

Caring, serving, donating, loving?

Reverse course. Reverse our checkbook. *Reverse the order.* Give first. Save second. Spend third. Give again.

To *reverse the order*—to change our spending habits—we must shift our focus. To others. Release our anxiety. Our doubt in what we have. Recognize our greatest obstacle is ourselves. Confident in our path to eternal life, we embrace deposits to our Spiritual Portfolio.

God's Checkbook commits to reverse.

Commits to tithe.

Commits to give generously.

Commits to *pay God first*.

This is not a *me* deal. This is an *our* deal. A community of believers. A community of followers. Sharing our thoughts, sharing our memories, sharing Jesus. Our gifts and tithes continue that early church. Continue what Jesus taught. His mission.

Our gifts provide community. Our gifts teach. Our gifts share. Our gifts offer a glimpse into what the early church was like.

Our community, our churches, provide an avenue for service and mission.

Our deposits are not to earn a reward, but to return a favor.

Return the blessings we have received.

These deposits are a response to God's love for us. A response to God's request that we love Him. That we love those whom He loves.

Along our journey to building and nurturing our Spiritual Portfolios, we bring Heaven to earth. Today. A richer, fuller life. Now. *A life which is selfless, emotionally sound, financially secure and spiritually focused.* A transformed life in Christ.

> It's no longer about making a living. We are making a life. We are restoring a life.

It's no longer about making a living. We are *making a life.* We are *restoring a life.*

A portfolio without limits and with everlasting tenure. True deposits from the heart. For others. For God. Our legacy. A portfolio funded and built on our view of what really matters in His Kingdom: loving God and loving others.

The more we give, the more we realize we can live without.

Generous giving recognizes what we have. Generous giving recognizes what God has provided. Generous giving pinches.

Pinches our pocketbook. Giving that hurts. Giving for those hurting. For those in pain.

Sacrifice today for tomorrow. Sacrifice comfort to care for others' pain.

Generous giving comes from a recognition that we need less and less in this life. We don't hoard, we share. We give it away. We use it for God's Kingdom.

With earthly finance—earthly markets, earthly portfolios— there are no guarantees. Strategies that work today may not work tomorrow.

Spiritual matters are entirely different.

"For God so loved the world that He gave His one and only Son, that whoever believes in Him shall not perish but have eternal life."[102]

His *past performance guarantees our future.*

Our Spiritual Portfolio is a witness. A witness to others of our faith in Jesus. Our Gifts, our Tithes, our Deeds, our Service. A testament to our earthly decision to follow Christ, to imitate Christ. An interest in bringing Heaven to earth. And acting on that interest today.

Our Spiritual Portfolio will live on in His memory.

As we embrace deposits to our Spiritual Portfolio, we must answer questions of ourselves. Much like questions I ask of my clients during our initial planning process.

What are your goals with your money? With your wealth? What legacy ideas do you have? What charitable intent do you seek?

How much do you need to live on? How much will you deposit annually?

What sort of risk are you willing to take?

How much time will you commit to review your portfolio once invested?

Questions and answers that ensure at the outset what we expect of each other. What we expect the portfolio to produce in results. In earnings. In dividends.

As we consider our deposits to Heaven, we must ask questions of ourselves, our faith and our commitment to the Kingdom. Questions that God might ask each of us as we launch this new investment program:

Do you love Me? Do you trust Me?

Do you love others? Will you serve Me by serving others?

Do you love the church? Will you provide for My church?

Do you view your wealth as Mine or yours?

Will you review your deposit allocation annually?

Will you see as I see?

Will you leave your comfort zone?

Will you erase your memory?

Will you imitate Christ?

To embrace our deposits, we must understand that *we ARE our Spiritual Portfolio*. And we must willingly embrace change. Embrace a new heart. A new self. To answer these questions, we must commit to deposit. As we deposit, we slowly receive rewards. As these rewards build in our hearts, we truly begin to answer God's most important questions: Do you love Me? Do you love others?

If your answer is "yes," then you are prepared to deposit. The rest is simple. Put that faith into action by making deposits to your Spiritual Portfolio. Brace yourself for a remarkable journey. In the now, and in the new beginning, when you hear Him say, "...Well done, good and faithful servant!"[103]

"Christ has no body now but yours, no hands but yours, no feet but yours. Yours are the eyes through which Christ's compassion must look out on the world. Yours are the feet with which He is to go about doing good. Yours are the hands with which He is to bless us now."[104] – Saint Teresa of Ávila

Epilogue

Lessons Learned

As I said at the beginning, I didn't set out to write this book, but it needed to be written. These lessons were not learned overnight. They were not learned perfectly. And in all truthfulness, they are still being learned to this day. Regardless of my imperfections, if I focus on what God would have me do in my daily life—to serve Him and those who He would have me serve—I will have accomplished more than the American dream, I will have fulfilled God's true vision for me and my family.

If I can leave you with anything, it would be a blessing that God helps you weather whatever storm you happen to be going through—both mentally, emotionally and spiritually—and that He give you a renewed sense of well-being, a sense of God's joy and grace rising from *what you have*, rather than what you don't. May you integrate these lessons into your daily living, and may they bless and change you as they have blessed and changed me.

1 I've Got It All...Now What?

Lesson: Greed ^(for God) is Good

You've got it all, and yet you find yourself empty. You strive for the American dream, yet you have lost meaning. Embrace your greed, but greed for something greater than yourself. Greed can be good. Greed for God.

2 Discover Your Spiritual Portfolio

Lesson: Focus On Your ~~Net~~ ^(Self) Worth

Open your heart to see God through actions for others. As Jesus did. As Jesus taught. Focus on others to reveal your true self worth. Discover your Spiritual Portfolio.

3 God's Calendar: Invest Time or Spend Time

Lesson: Time ^(for God) is Money

Focus on God's calendar. Deposits of time. Invested in others. Love who He loves. Emulate Him in service. With your life centered on Jesus, time for God is money.

4 Spiritual Deposit: Good Deeds

Lesson: It's All About ~~Me~~ *You* ^

Unselfish acts towards others.   Unconditional service. Compassion and mercy to those in need. Good Deeds. Jesus did it. So should you. Tell yourself, "It's not about ME, it's about YOU." It's about someone else.

5 Spiritual Deposit: Big Deeds

Lesson: ~~First~~ *Last* ^ in This World

Change your perception. Lose your agenda. Go on a mission trip. Planned in advance. Big Deeds. Make your mission, your service, routine. Serve those who may be last in this world but will be first in the next.

6 God's Checkbook: To Give or Not To Give

Lesson: Balance Your *Spiritual* ^ Checkbook

Stop comparing. Shift focus. Give up the pursuit. Be content. Balance your Spiritual Checkbook by recognizing the blessings God has provided. Treat your bank balance as God's Checkbook.

7   Reverse the Order

Lesson: Pay ~~Yourself~~ ^God^ First

Commit to reverse your order of consumption. Commit to others. Commit to tithe. Commit to give generously. Pay God first. Reverse course. Reverse your checkbook. Reverse the order. Give First. Save Second. Spend Third. Give Again.

8   Spiritual Deposit: Faithful Gifts

Lesson: Invest In ~~Your~~ ^Our^ Future

This is not a *you* deal. This is an *our* deal. A community of believers. A community of faith. Our gifts teach. Our gifts share. Our faithful gifts are not to earn a reward, but to return a favor. Invest in our future. Our mission.

9   Spiritual Deposit: Generous Gifts

Lesson: Make a ~~Living~~ ^Life^

Generous giving pinches. Giving that hurts. For those hurting. Sacrifice today for tomorrow. Sacrifice comfort to care for others' pain. As you make a living, strive to make a life for yourself and others in God's Kingdom.

10 Portfolio Review

Lesson: Past Performance ~~Does Not Equal~~ *Equals* ^
Future Results

God so loved the world that He gave us Jesus. To imitate. To emulate. To offer eternal life. His performance guarantees your future. Review your portfolio of Gifts, Tithes, Deeds and Service. Your witness. Your testament to an earthly decision to follow Christ.

11 Restore Life

Lesson: You Are Your ~~Financial~~ *Spiritual* ^ Portfolio

You ARE your Spiritual Portfolio. Your Jesus attitude. An attitude of kindness and caring toward others. Embrace change. Put your faith into action. Give. Serve. Brace yourself for a restored life, and a remarkable journey.

Endnotes

Introduction & Acknowledgments

[1] Shane Claiborne, *The Irresistible Revolution: Living As An Ordinary Radical.* Copyright © 2006 by The Simple Way. (Grand Rapids, Michigan: Zondervan)

Chapter One

[2] Ken Blanchard and Phil Hodges, *Lead Like Jesus: Lessons from the Greatest Leadership Role Model of All Time.* Copyright © 2005 by Ken Blanchard and Phil Hodges. (Nashville, Tennessee: Thomas Nelson, Inc.)

[3] Brian D. McLaren, *The Secret Message of Jesus: Uncovering the Truth That Could Change Everything.* Copyright © 2006 by Brian D. McLaren. (Nashville, Tennessee: Thomas Nelson, Inc.)

Chapter Two

[4] Rob Bell, *Sex God: Exploring the Endless Connections Between Sexuality and Spirituality.* Copyright © 2007 by Rob Bell. (Grand Rapids, Michigan: Zondervan)

[5] Matthew 25:21

[6] Luke 12:33-34

[7] Romans 5:1-2

[8] Luke 12:33-34

[9] Luke 12:48

[10] *AARP Thoughts on Afterlife Among U.S. Adults 50+*, Conducted for *AARP The Magazine*. June 2007. Report written by Jean Koppen, Senior Research Advisor and Gretchen Anderson, Research Analyst National Member Research. Survey conducted by International Communications Research. Copyright © AARP

[11] Table 2. Projections of the Population by Selected Age Groups and Sex for the United States: 2010 to 2050 (NP2008-T2). Source: Population Division, U.S. Census Bureau. Release Date: August 14, 2008. www.census.gov

[12] Table 3. Percent Distribution of the Projected Population by Selected Age Groups and Sex for the United States: 2010 to 2050 (NP2008-T3). Source: Population Division, U.S. Census Bureau. Release Date: August 14, 2008. www.census.gov

[13] Society of Actuaries RP-2000 Mortality Tables. Copyright © 2000 – 2001 by the Society of Actuaries, Schaumburg, Illinois. www.soa.org

[14] Acts 9:1-19

Chapter Three

[15] Marcus J. Borg, *The Heart of Christianity: Rediscovering a Life of Faith*. Copyright © 2003 by Marcus J. Borg. (New York, New York: HarperSanFrancisco, A Division of HarperCollins Publishers, Inc.)

[16] Ken Blanchard and Phil Hodges, *Lead Like Jesus: Lessons from the Greatest Leadership Role Model of All Time*. Copyright © 2005 by Ken Blanchard and Phil Hodges. (Nashville, Tennessee: Thomas Nelson, Inc.)

[17] Mark 10:51

[18] Mark 10:52

[19] Matthew 5:3

[20] 1 Corinthians 13:4-7

[21] Bureau of Labor Statistics release titled *Volunteering in the United States, 2006* – News Release from the United States Department of Labor, Washington, D.C., January 10, 2007. USDL 07-0019

[22] Bureau of Labor Statistics release titled *Volunteering in the United States, 2006* – News Release from the United States Department of Labor, Washington, D.C., January 10, 2007. USDL 07-0019

[23] Bureau of Labor Statistics release titled *Volunteering in the United States, 2006* – News Release from the United States Department of Labor, Washington, D.C., January 10, 2007. USDL 07-0019

[24] To learn more about Habitat for Humanity, visit www.habitat.org

[25] Randy Alcorn, *Heaven*. Copyright © 2004 by Eternal Perspective Ministries. (Carol Stream, Illinois: Tyndale House Publishers, Inc.)

Chapter Four

[26] Rob Bell, *Velvet Elvis: Repainting the Christian Faith*. Copyright © 2005 by Rob Bell. (Grand Rapids, Michigan: Zondervan)

²⁷ John 15:17

²⁸ Dr. James C. Denison, *Our First Amendment Right to Recite the First Amendment.* God Issues devotional dated September 26, 2007. Copyright © 2007 by Dr. James C. Denison and www.GodIssues.com

²⁹ Matthew 6:30

Chapter Five
³⁰ To learn more about some of the work being done in Juarez, Mexico, visit Amor Ministries at www.amor.org

³¹ David L. Goetz, *Death by Suburb: How to Keep the Suburbs From Killing Your Soul.* Copyright © 2006 by David L. Goetz. (New York, New York: HarperSanFrancisco, A Division of HarperCollins Publishers, Inc.)

³² Mother Teresa, *Come Be My Light: The Private Writings of the Saint of Calcutta.* Copyright © 2007 by The Mother Teresa Center. Edited and with Commentary by Brian Kolodiejchuk, M.C. (New York, New York: Doubleday, an imprint of The Doubleday Broadway Publishing Group, a division of Random House, Inc.)

³³ Luke 22:27

³⁴ Rob Bell, *Velvet Elvis: Repainting the Christian Faith.* Copyright © 2005 by Rob Bell. (Grand Rapids, Michigan: Zondervan)

³⁵ Matthew 19:30

³⁶ Rob Bell, *Velvet Elvis: Repainting the Christian Faith.* Copyright © 2005 by Rob Bell. (Grand Rapids, Michigan: Zondervan)

³⁷ Tom Wright, *John for Everyone, Part Two Chapters 11-21.* Copyright © 2002, 2004 by Nicholas Thomas Wright. (London, England: Society for Promoting Christian Knowledge; Louisville, Kentucky: Westminster John Knox Press)

³⁸ Ephesians 6:8

³⁹ Great Day of Service held at Highland Park United Methodist Church, Dallas, Texas www.HPUMC.org

⁴⁰ Community Partners of Dallas - The Rainbow Room. www.communitypartnersdallas.org

⁴¹ To learn more about meal delivery visit The Visiting Nurse Association of Texas www.vnatexas.org or Meals on Wheels Association of America www.mowaa.org

Chapter Six

[42] Donald Miller, *Blue Like Jazz: Nonreligious Thoughts on Christian Spirituality.* Copyright © 2003 by Donald Miller. (Nashville, Tennessee: Thomas Nelson, Inc.)

[43] Luke 12:34

[44] Gifts of Grace 2007 Mission, Highland Park United Methodist Church, Dallas, Texas www.HPUMC.org

[45] For more information on SoupMobile, visit www.soupmobile.org

[46] For more information on North Texas Food Bank, visit www.ntxfoodbank.org

[47] For more information on Agape Clinic, visit www.agapeclinic.org

[48] For more information on the Evangelical Methodist Church, visit www.costaricamissionprojects.com

[49] For more information on the Malaria Net Mission, visit www.nothingbutnets.net/

[50] Marcus J. Borg, *The Heart of Christianity: Rediscovering a Life of Faith.* Copyright © 2003 by Marcus J. Borg. (New York, New York: HarperSanFrancisco, A Division of HarperCollins Publishers, Inc.)

Chapter Seven

[51] C.S. Lewis, *Mere Christianity.* Copyright © 1952 by C.S. Lewis Pte. Ltd. Copyright renewed © 1980 by C.S. Lewis Pte. Ltd. (New York, New York: HarperSanFrancisco, A Division of HarperCollins Publishers, Inc.)

[52] David L. Goetz, *Death by Suburb: How to Keep the Suburbs From Killing Your Soul.* Copyright © 2006 by David L. Goetz. (New York, New York: HarperSanFrancisco, A Division of HarperCollins Publishers, Inc.)

[53] Luke 16:11

[54] Dallas Willard, *The Divine Conspiracy: Rediscovering Our Hidden Life in God.* Copyright © 1998 by Dallas Willard. (London, England: Fount Paperbacks; New York, New York: HarperSanFrancisco, A Division of HarperCollins Publishers, Inc.)

[55] Dallas Willard, *The Divine Conspiracy: Rediscovering Our Hidden Life in God.* Copyright © 1998 by Dallas Willard. (London, England: Fount Paperbacks; New York, New York: HarperSanFrancisco, A Division of HarperCollins Publishers, Inc.)

⁵⁶ 2 Corinthians 9:6-7

Chapter Eight

⁵⁷ www.GenerousGiving.org Position Statements on Stewardship-Related Issues. Statement #9: The Tithe. 2 Corinthians 9:7; Acts 4: 32-37. Copyright © 2000 – 2006 by Generous Giving (www.generousgiving.org)

⁵⁸ Acts 4: 32-34

⁵⁹ Tom Wright, *John for Everyone, Part Two Chapters 11-21.* Copyright © 2002, 2004 by Nicholas Thomas Wright. (London, England: Society for Promoting Christian Knowledge; Louisville, Kentucky: Westminster John Knox Press)

⁶⁰ www.GenerousGiving.org Position Statements on Stewardship-Related Issues. Statement #9: The Tithe. 2 Corinthians 8:9; John 12:34; 1 John 3:16-18; 2 Corinthians 9:7. Copyright © 2000 – 2006 by Generous Giving (www.generousgiving.org)

⁶¹ Brian D. McLaren, *A New Kind of Christian: A Tale of Two Friends on a Spiritual Journey.* Copyright © 2001 by Brian D. McLaren. (San Francisco, California: Jossey-Bass, A Wiley Imprint)

⁶² To learn more about meal delivery visit The Visiting Nurse Association of Texas www.vnatexas.org or Meals on Wheels Association of America www.mowaa.org

⁶³ To learn more about soup kitchens via The SoupMobile visit www.soupmobile.org

⁶⁴ To learn more about affordable housing via Builders of Hope visit www.buildersofhopecdc.com

⁶⁵ To learn more about prison ministry via the Prison Entrepreneurship Program visit www.pep.org

⁶⁶ Rob Bell, *Velvet Elvis: Repainting the Christian Faith.* Copyright © 2005 by Rob Bell. (Grand Rapids, Michigan: Zondervan)

⁶⁷ Rob Bell, *Velvet Elvis: Repainting the Christian Faith.* Copyright © 2005 by Rob Bell. (Grand Rapids, Michigan: Zondervan)

⁶⁸ C.S. Lewis, *Mere Christianity.* Copyright © 1952 by C.S. Lewis Pte. Ltd. Copyright renewed © 1980 by C.S. Lewis Pte. Ltd. (New York, New York: HarperSanFrancisco, A Division of HarperCollins Publishers, Inc.)

⁶⁹ Marcus J. Borg, *The Heart of Christianity: Rediscovering a Life of*

Faith. Copyright © 2003 by Marcus J. Borg. (New York, New York: HarperSanFrancisco, A Division of HarperCollins Publishers, Inc.)

Chapter Nine

[70]   Matthew 6:21

[71]   David L. Goetz, *Death by Suburb: How to Keep the Suburbs From Killing Your Soul.* Copyright © 2006 by David L. Goetz. (New York, New York: HarperSanFrancisco, A Division of HarperCollins Publishers, Inc.)

[72]   C.S. Lewis, *Mere Christianity.* Copyright © 1952 by C.S. Lewis Pte. Ltd. Copyright renewed © 1980 by C.S. Lewis Pte. Ltd. (New York, New York: HarperSanFrancisco, A Division of HarperCollins Publishers, Inc.) Author Note: C.S. Lewis attributes this quote to George MacDonald

[73]   C.S. Lewis, *Mere Christianity.* Copyright © 1952 by C.S. Lewis Pte. Ltd. Copyright renewed © 1980 by C.S. Lewis Pte. Ltd. (New York, New York: HarperSanFrancisco, A Division of HarperCollins Publishers, Inc.)

[74]   C.S. Lewis, *Mere Christianity.* Copyright © 1952 by C.S. Lewis Pte. Ltd. Copyright renewed © 1980 by C.S. Lewis Pte. Ltd. (New York, New York: HarperSanFrancisco, A Division of HarperCollins Publishers, Inc.)

[75]   *Giving USA™ 2008: The Annual Report on Philanthropy for the Year 2007 (53rd Annual Issue)*, a publication of Giving USA Foundation™, researched and written by the Center on Philanthropy at Indiana University. Copyright © 2008 by Giving USA Foundation™. www.givingusa.org

[76]   DeNavas-Walt, Carmen, Bernadette D. Proctor, and Jessica Smith, U.S. Census Bureau, Current Population Reports, P60-233, *Income, Poverty, and Health Insurance Coverage in the United Sates: 2006*, U.S. Government Printing Office, Washington, DC, 2007. U.S. Census Bureau News Release, August 28, 2007, *Household Income Rise, Poverty Rate Declines, Number of Uninsured Up.*

[77]   *TNS Reports Record Breaking Number of Millionaires in the USA* from its annual Affluent Market Research program (AMRP), January 5, 2007. Copyright © 1998 – 2009 by Taylor Nelson Sofres, A Kantar Group Company. www.tns-global.com/

[78]   Randy Alcorn, *The Treasure Principle: Unlocking the Secret of Joyful Giving.* Copyright © 2001 by Eternal Perspective Ministries. (Colorado Springs, Colorado: Multnomah Publishers, a Division of Random House, Inc.; LifeChange Books)

[79]   U.S. Department of Labor, Bureau of Labor Statistics, Issues in

Labor Statistics, *Spending Patterns by Age*. Summary 00-16 August 2000 (Consumer Expenditure Survey, 1998.)

[80]   Rollyn H. Samp, J.D., *The Final Tithe: A Christian Approach to Estate Planning*. Copyright © 2005 by Rushmore House Publishing A/D/O New Capital Development, Inc. (Sioux Falls, South Dakota: Rushmore House Publishing)

[81]   United Nations Department of Economic and Social Affairs (DESA), *The Millennium Development Goals Report 2008*. Copyright © 2008 by United Nations. Anne Ellinger and Christopher Ellinger, *Why Don't Affluent Baby Boomers Give More Money Away?* AlterNet, June 21, 2007. Copyright © 2007 by Independent Media Institute. www.alternet.org

Chapter Ten

[82]   Randy Alcorn, *Heaven*. Copyright © 2004 by Eternal Perspective Ministries. (Carol Stream, Illinois: Tyndale House Publishers, Inc.) 2 Corinthians 5:10, Matthew 12:36

[83]   *AARP Thoughts on Afterlife Among U.S. Adults 50+*, Conducted for *AARP The Magazine*. June 2007. Report written by Jean Koppen, Senior Research Advisor and Gretchen Anderson, Research Analyst National Member Research. Survey conducted by International Communications Research. Copyright © AARP

[84]   Donald Miller, *Searching for God Knows What*. Copyright © 2004 by Donald Miller. (Nashville, Tennessee: Thomas Nelson, Inc.)

[85]   Donald Miller, *Searching for God Knows What*. Copyright © 2004 by Donald Miller. (Nashville, Tennessee: Thomas Nelson, Inc.)

[86]   C.S. Lewis, *Mere Christianity.* Copyright © 1952 by C.S. Lewis Pte. Ltd. Copyright renewed © 1980 by C.S. Lewis Pte. Ltd. (New York, New York: HarperSanFrancisco, A Division of HarperCollins Publishers, Inc.)

[87]   To learn more about Outreach Camps for Kids, explore Kids Across America @ www.kidsacrossamerica.org

[88]   To learn more about prison ministry, explore Prison Entrepreneurship Program @ www.pep.org

[89]   Community Partners of Dallas - The Rainbow Room. www.communitypartnersdallas.org

[90]   Rob Bell, *Sex God: Exploring the Endless Connections Between Sexuality and Spirituality.* Copyright © 2007 by Rob Bell. (Grand Rapids, Michigan: Zondervan)

91 To learn more about Outreach Camps for Kids, explore Kids Across America @ www.kidsacrossamerica.org

Chapter Eleven

92 Bob Buford, *Halftime: Changing Your Game Plan from Success to Significance.* Copyright © 1994 by Robert P. Buford. (Grand Rapids, Michigan: Zondervan)

93 Marcus J. Borg, *The Heart of Christianity: Rediscovering a Life of Faith.* Copyright © 2003 by Marcus J. Borg. (New York, New York: HarperSanFrancisco, A Division of HarperCollins Publishers, Inc.)

94 1 John 4:19

95 1 John 4:11

96 1 John 4:16

97 John 14:12

98 John 3:30

99 C.S. Lewis, *Mere Christianity.* Copyright © 1952 by C.S. Lewis Pte. Ltd. Copyright renewed © 1980 by C.S. Lewis Pte. Ltd. (New York, New York: HarperSanFrancisco, A Division of HarperCollins Publishers, Inc.)

100 Randy Alcorn, *Heaven.* Copyright © 2004 by Eternal Perspective Ministries. (Carol Stream, Illinois: Tyndale House Publishers, Inc.) 1 Corinthians 3:14

101 *Open the Eyes of My Heart* Author: Paul Baloche. Copyright © 1997 Integrity's Hosanna! Music. Catalog: Integrity's Hosanna! Music. Administrator: Integrity Music, Inc.

102 John 3:16

103 Matthew 25:21

104 Saint Teresa of Ávila, *Christ Has No Body.*

All Scripture references, unless otherwise indicated, are taken from *Life Application® Study Bible*, New International Version edition, published jointly by Tyndale House Publishers, Inc. and Zondervan Publishing House. The Bible text used in this edition is the *Holy Bible*, New International Version®. Life Application® Study Bible Copyright © 1988, 1989, 1990, 1991 by Tyndale House Publishers, Inc., Wheaton, IL. All rights reserved.

About the Author

Brandon Pope has spent the past 20 years providing investment and financial counseling services for close to 100 of the nations' wealthiest high net-worth individuals, families, trusts, estates and foundations. Building and advising close to $1 Billion in investment portfolio assets and total personal fortunes exceeding $3 Billion, Brandon brings a unique perspective to spiritual investment planning, giving and wealth.

Brandon's tenure began advising clients of the international accounting and consulting firms of KPMG & PriceWaterhouseCoopers. Brandon currently advises clients with the premier Wall Street investment management firm

Bernstein Global Wealth Management, a unit of AllianceBernstein L.P., whose combined assets total close to $500 Billion.

Mr. Pope received his Bachelor of Science in Business Administration and his Master of Accounting degrees from the University of North Carolina at Chapel Hill. Mr. Pope is truly a student of his profession, gathering the following designations and licenses: Certified Public Accountant (CPA), Certified Financial Planner™ (CFP®), Personal Financial Specialist (PFS) and Chartered Life Underwriter (CLU®). Brandon has served on numerous charitable boards, charitable foundations, has published several articles and is an active speaker on faith and financial planning topics.

Brandon, age 43, is married to his adoring wife of 18 years, Maria, has a son Jackson, 14, and daughter Rachel, 10. Brandon's church home is Cornerstone, the contemporary worship community of Highland Park United Methodist Church located in Dallas, Texas, where his family has been a resident since 1993.

www.BrandonKPope.com